OCCASIONAL PAPER **232**

China's Growth and Integration into the World Economy

Prospects and Challenges

Edited by Eswar Prasad

With contributions from
Steven Barnett, Nicolas Blancher, Ray Brooks, Annalisa Fedelino,
Tarhan Feyzioğlu, Thomas Rumbaugh, Raju Jan Singh, and Tao Wang

INTERNATIONAL MONETARY FUND
Washington DC
2004

Production: IMF Multimedia Services Division
Typesetting: Choon Lee
Figures: Theodore F. Peters, Jr.

Cataloging-in-Publication Data

China's growth and integration into the world economy: prospects and challenges/edited by Eswar Prasad; with contributions from Steven Barnett . . . [et al.]—Washington, D.C.: International Monetary Fund, 2004.

p. cm. — (Occasional paper, 0251-6365; 232)

Includes bibliographical references.
ISBN 1-58906-258-2

1. China—Foreign economic relations. 2. Prices—China. 3. Foreign exchange—China. 4. Banks and banking—China. 5. Labor market—China. I. Prasad, Eswar. II. Barnett, Steven (Steven Alan). III. Occasional paper (International Monetary Fund); no. 232.

HF1604.C45 2004

Price: US$25.00
(US$22.00 to full-time faculty members and
students at universities and colleges)

Please send orders to:
International Monetary Fund, Publication Services
700 19th Street, N.W., Washington, D.C. 20431, U.S.A.
Tel.: (202) 623-7430   Telefax: (202) 623-7201
E-mail: publications@imf.org
Internet: http://www.imf.org

recycled paper

Contents

Figures

The following symbols have been used throughout this paper:

. . . to indicate that data are not available;

— to indicate that the figure is zero or less than half the final digit shown, or that the item does not exist;

– between years or months (e.g., 2001–02 or January–June) to indicate the years or months covered, including the beginning and ending years or months;

/ between years (e.g., 2001/02) to indicate a fiscal (financial) year.

"n.a." means not applicable.

"Billion" means a thousand million.

Minor discrepancies between constituent figures and totals are due to rounding.

The term "country," as used in this paper, does not in all cases refer to a territorial entity that is a state as understood by international law and practice; the term also covers some territorial entities that are not states, but for which statistical data are maintained and provided internationally on a separate and independent basis.

Preface

This Occasional Paper provides an overview of analytical work done by IMF staff as background for the 2002 and 2003 Article IV Consultations with the People's Republic of China.

The authors would like to express their deep appreciation for the valuable guidance provided by Steven Dunaway, the IMF's mission chief for China during this period. They also thank David Burton and Wanda Tseng for their encouragement and advice. The authors are grateful to the Chinese authorities for the information that they provided and for the extensive discussions and comments that helped sharpen the analysis and presentation in this paper. Ioana Hussiada provided research assistance for this project; Yuko Kobayashi and Carolina Klein handled the preparation of the manuscript; and Esha Ray of the External Relations Department coordinated production of the publication.

The opinions expressed in this paper are solely those of its authors and do not necessarily reflect the views of the International Monetary Fund, its Executive Directors, or the Chinese authorities.

Abbreviations and Acronyms

ABC	Agricultural Bank of China
ASEAN	Association of South-East Asian Nations
ATC	Agreement on Textiles and Clothing
BOC	Bank of China
CARs	Capital adequacy ratios
CBRC	China Banking Regulatory Commission
CCB	China Construction Bank
CNAO	National Audit Office of the People's Republic of China
CPI	Consumer price index
EIT	Enterprise income tax
EMBI	JP Morgan Emerging Market Bond Index
EU	European Union
FDI	Foreign direct investment
FFEs	Foreign-funded enterprises
GDP	Gross domestic product
GTAP	Global Trade Analysis Project
ICBC	Industrial and Commercial Bank of China
ILO	International Labor Organization
JSCBs	Joint-stock commercial banks
MFN	Most-favored-nation
MOLSS	Ministry of Labor and Social Services
NBS	National Bureau of Statistics
NEER	Nominal effective exchange rate
NFA	Net foreign assets
NIEs	Newly industrialized economies
NPL	Nonperforming loan
NTBs	Nontariff barriers
OECD	Organization for Economic Cooperation and Development
OLS	Ordinary least squares
PBC	People's Bank of China
PPI	Producer price index
PPP	Purchasing power parity
RCCs	Rural credit cooperatives
RECs	Reemployment centers
REER	Real effective exchange rate
RPI	Retail price index
SCBs	State-owned commercial banks
SITC	Standard International Trade Classification
SOE	State-owned enterprise
TRIMs	Trade-Related Investment Measures
TRIPs	Trade-Related Aspects of Intellectual Property Rights
TSA	Treasury single account
TVEs	Town and village enterprises
ULC	Unit labor costs
UNCTAD	United Nations Conference on Trade and Development
VAR	Vector autoregression
VAT	Value-added tax
WTO	World Trade Organization

I Overview

Eswar Prasad and Thomas Rumbaugh

China's transformation into a dynamic private-sector-led economy and its integration into the global economy have been among the most dramatic economic developments of recent decades. Indeed, China's growth performance over the last two decades has been spectacular, with GDP growth averaging almost 8 percent. China now ranks as the sixth largest economy in the world (at market exchange rates). The expansion of China's role in the world trading system has been no less remarkable, with its overall share in world trade rising from less than 1 percent in 1979 to about 6 percent in 2003.

There are strong prospects that China's rapid economic growth and trade expansion could be sustained well into the future. However, a number of macroeconomic and structural vulnerabilities need to be addressed for this potential to be fully realized. Given the size and complexity of the Chinese economy, many of these reform challenges are interrelated. China's traditional approach to reform has been incremental (Box 1.1) but, in view of its rapid opening up to the world economy, a more concerted and multifaceted approach to the reform process will be crucial to maintain rapid growth and manage the challenges associated with the process of global integration. This Occasional Paper provides an overview of some of the key aspects of China's recent growth and integration with the global economy and discusses some of the main policy challenges that lie ahead.

Rapidly Expanding International Trade

The expansion of its international trade has been a particularly noteworthy aspect of China's rising prominence in the world economy. China's exports and imports have grown at an average rate of 15 percent each year since 1979, compared with a 7 percent annual expansion of world trade over the same period. This process has been facilitated by trade reforms and the general opening of the economy that have led to a surge in foreign direct investment (FDI) and increased integration with the global trad-

ing system. Interestingly, as discussed in Section II, the rapid expansion of China's trade thus far is not unprecedented in either its scope or speed. Other Asian economies such as Japan, Korea, and the newly industrialized emerging economies of Asia were able to maintain even higher export growth rates, on average, for about a 30-year period. This international experience implies that China could maintain relatively strong export growth for a number of years. Given China's large population and still substantial development potential (as reflected by its current per capita income of only $1,060), China could have a bigger impact on the global economy than the other economies mentioned above.

China's trade expansion in part reflects greater specialization in production within the Asian region, with China now serving as the final processing and assembly platform for a large quantity of imports going from other Asian countries to Western countries through China (see Prasad and Rumbaugh, 2003). These changes have resulted in a shift in China's bilateral trade balances, with its increasing trade surpluses with Western industrial countries being offset by rising trade deficits with many Asian countries. Reflecting its growing prominence and rising appetite for imports (including for meeting domestic demand), China has been an important source of growth for the world economy during the recent global slowdown. During 2001–03, China accounted for about 24 percent of world growth (using purchasing-power-parity-based GDP). China's imports are growing rapidly from all trading partners and it is now the third largest importer of developing countries' exports after the United States and the European Union. China has even contributed to the recent strength in world commodity prices; it is now the world's largest importer of copper and steel, and among the largest importers of other raw materials, including iron ore and aluminum.

While China's integration into the global trading system is likely to benefit both the global and regional economies, there will no doubt be some short-run distributional effects across countries. The

Box 1.1. China's Approach to Economic Reform

For three decades after the 1949 revolution, China followed a policy of socialist economic development based primarily on the centrally directed allocation of resources through administrative means. By the late 1970s, this approach was increasingly recognized as being untenable and unsustainable, and an overhaul of the economic system was initiated.

China's approach to economic reform has been gradual and incremental, without any detailed "blueprint" guiding the process. This incremental approach is best depicted in a metaphor attributed to Deng Xiaoping as "crossing the river by feeling the stones under the feet" and is still applicable to many of the reforms being carried out by China today.

This incremental approach has been characterized by the following features. First, reforms tend to be undertaken first on a pilot or experimental basis in some localities before they are applied to the whole country. In the view of the authorities, this minimizes disruptions to the economy, allows deficient policies to be modified based on experience, and provides time to build the necessary institutions for full implementation. Second, another strategy frequently employed has been the use of intermediate mechanisms to smooth the transition to a market-oriented economy. One example of this is the setting up of Special Economic Zones in the early 1980s as a way of gradually introducing foreign capital and technology. Finally, the Chinese leadership has consistently tried to preserve the socialist character of the economy while introducing market-oriented reforms. For example, even though policies have been conducive to the rapid growth of the nonstate sector, state enterprise reform has been gradual with no signs of a mass privatization strategy for large and medium-sized enterprises as pursued by other transition economies.

Economic reform since the late 1970s can roughly be divided into five phases.[1] In the first phase (1978–84),

the organization of farming was decentralized to the household level, agricultural prices were raised, and some state-owned enterprises were allowed to retain profits as an incentive for good performance. The success of the rural reforms encouraged the authorities to introduce further reforms to the urban industrial sectors in a second phase (1984–88), including some liberalization in enterprise pricing and wage setting, introduction of enterprise taxation, and breakup of the monobank system. Fourteen major cities in the coastal areas were also opened up to foreign trade and investment.

The third (1988–91) and fourth (1992–1997) phases continued the reform process, but were also characterized by the lack of effective institutions and instruments for macroeconomic management. Inflation increased considerably after price liberalization and, in the third phase, the authorities recentralized many price controls and administered sharp contractionary policies to control double-digit inflation, This was effective in stabilizing prices but also produced a sharp slowing in the economy, mounting losses in state-owned enterprises, and rapid increases in interenterprise debt that threatened to further destabilize the macroeconomic situation. In the fourth phase, stimulative policies returned, leading the economy into another growth cycle.

More fundamentally, however, the highlight of the fourth phase was in 1992, when the Communist Party formally embraced Deng Xiaoping's view that the market system was not incompatible with the ideals of socialism and called for the establishment of a socialist market economy. This provided essential political support for major decisions to restructure the role and function of government, as well as the development of plans to speed up enterprise, financial, and social reforms and set the stage for a more fundamental "globalization" of the Chinese economy, in a fifth phase (1998 to present). This most recent phase has been characterized by a broader and more general opening up of the economy, including more broad-based trade liberalization and comprehensive commitments in the context of accession to the World Trade Organization to open the agricultural and services sectors of the economy.

[1]For a further description of the earlier reform periods see Bell, Khor, and Kochhar (1993) and Tseng and others (1994).

countries most likely to benefit from the expansion of China's trade include exporters of capital- and resource-intensive products, while countries that specialize in labor-intensive exports similar to those of China will have to undergo significant adjustments to increased competition from China. Trade expansion will also pose some domestic challenges within China itself. Expanding trade could increase regional income disparities, while foreign competition could aggravate social pressures arising from job dislocation and rising unemployment.

Price Dynamics

As a result of increased integration with the global economy and continued domestic price liberalization, prices in China are increasingly market determined and traded goods' prices have achieved substantial convergence with international prices. Even though not all prices in China are market determined, understanding the causes of variations in aggregate prices is important for domestic macroeconomic policy management. Characteristic of the challenges of modeling inflation dynamics in China, it has experienced two recent episodes of mild deflation (1998–2000 and 2001–02) despite sustained high output growth.

The analysis in Section III suggests that supply-related factors have been key determinants of recent price dynamics in China, especially during the recent deflationary episodes. Some of the supply factors are transitory, including the declines in commodity prices at the beginning of each of these episodes and restraints on administrative price increases. There are also longer-term factors on the supply side, such as productivity gains from strong investment, a series of tariff reductions, state enterprise reform, and adoption of new technologies that continue to exert significant downward pressures on prices. As discussed further below, a large labor surplus in rural areas and excess capacity in some state enterprises are also acting to keep costs and prices down. On the other hand, strong growth of monetary aggregates has supported price increases, particularly in 2003.

Real Exchange Rate Fluctuations

A great deal of recent debate has focused attention on China's exchange rate regime. China maintains a de facto fixed exchange rate regime, with the renminbi linked to the U.S. dollar within a narrow trading band. China's strong export growth, expanding market shares in major trading partner countries, and rapid accumulation of reserves have raised questions about whether the renminbi's link to the U.S. dollar may have resulted in an undervaluation of the currency. However, estimating a currency's "equilibrium exchange rate" is a very complicated matter, with the difficulties greatly compounded in the case of a developing country like China that is undergoing substantial structural change. Indeed, as the analysis in Section IV shows, existing techniques provide a very wide range of estimates of the equilibrium exchange rate from a medium-term perspective, and each of these estimates is in turn sensitive to various assumptions.

The analysis also shows how different sources of shocks could affect the medium-term path of the exchange rate. The currency's value will be inexorably linked to the ongoing structural reforms of the economy, and will reflect further opening of domestic markets to foreign goods and services in line with World Trade Organization (WTO) commitments. Moreover, the medium-term movement of the exchange rate will depend on the nature and pace of liberalization of capital controls. Thus, discussions about attaining a particular level of the exchange rate may be less productive than focusing on the broader benefits of exchange rate flexibility for China.

Fiscal Policy

As the economy opens up, domestic macroeconomic policies will have a prominent role in reducing vulnerability to external shocks. For an economy with a tightly managed exchange rate, fiscal policy is therefore of considerable importance. With relatively low explicit government debt (26 percent of GDP) and a modest budget deficit (3 percent of GDP), China clearly does not face immediate concerns of fiscal sustainability. However, as discussed in Section V, the government faces a number of possible future obligations associated with potential losses in the state-dominated banking system, the future funding requirements of the pension system, and rising expenditure pressures, especially for education, health, and other social programs. Resolving the substantial quasi-fiscal liabilities poses a significant medium-term challenge. This challenge could increase substantially if macroeconomic conditions, especially growth, were to become less favorable or if structural reforms were not forceful enough to prevent the accumulation of new contingent liabilities. This highlights the urgency of undertaking structural reforms since many of these liabilities could otherwise pose an even greater burden in the future.

Another aspect of the public finances that is relevant to macroeconomic outcomes is related to intergovernmental fiscal relations. The 1994 fiscal decentralization reforms succeeded in raising government revenue and in increasing the share going to the central government, and appear to have been effective in stimulating growth at the provincial level. However, this growth has been unbalanced and income disparities across provinces have widened over time. Center-local fiscal relations have not been effective in reducing these disparities, especially since the transfer mechanism from the center to the provinces is not sufficiently progressive. Furthermore, the resources available to provinces, especially the poorer ones, have not kept pace with their rising expenditure mandates. This has led subnational governments to rely on indirect sources of financing and the associated creation of implicit liabilities at the local level poses significant fiscal risks. Section VI discusses the decentralization reforms and their effects, and reviews the main challenges that lie ahead in improving the structure of intergovernmental fiscal relations.

Banking System Reform

Financial intermediation in China occurs mainly through the banking system. State-owned banks dominate the banking system and are the main official source of financing for companies, since the stock market is relatively thin and there is no corporate bond market. Banks have a crucial role in intermediating the substantial amount of private saving in China, which is estimated to be around one-third of total household income. Bank lending has supported the high level of investment growth, which has made an important contribution to China's growth performance in recent years. Stability of the banking system is therefore crucial for promoting sustained growth. Section VII discusses the financial sector reforms that have been undertaken recently and highlights the remaining challenges. The urgency of financial sector reforms has increased as domestic banks will need to be prepared to face intense competition when, under WTO accession commitments, the financial sector is opened up to foreign banks in 2006.

Unemployment

Many of the inefficiencies in the Chinese economy are ultimately manifested in labor market outcomes. Unemployment and "underemployment" of a significant portion of the rural population remain pressing concerns as the economy adjusts to the effects of state-owned enterprise (SOE) reforms and WTO accession. Section VIII surveys recent labor market developments and indicates that, even with strong output growth, the unemployment problem is in fact likely to worsen over the next few years due to restructuring in the rural and state enterprise sectors.

How soon the unemployment problem will be brought under control will depend in large part on the degree to which the reforms described earlier are undertaken. To mitigate social pressures as labor is shifted from agriculture to other parts of the economy and from the state sector to the private sector, further progress will be needed in strengthening the social safety net, including the pension system, unemployment insurance, health care, and the minimum living allowance. Needless to say, these measures will have fiscal implications as well, again reflecting the interconnectedness of required reforms on various fronts.

The Outlook

China's economy has good potential for sustained robust growth over the medium term, based on its attractiveness as a destination for FDI, a high domestic saving rate, underlying improvements in productivity stemming from reduced barriers to both internal and external trade, and significant surplus labor. But fulfilling its potential for high growth and continued integration with the global economy will depend largely on successful management of the diverse set of financial and social risks that China faces. This, in turn, will depend crucially on the pace and effectiveness of core macroeconomic and structural reforms. Implementing a broad and concerted reform agenda, and doing so in an expeditious manner, is indeed the crucial challenge facing Chinese policymakers.

II International Trade and the Challenges of WTO Accession

Thomas Rumbaugh and Nicolas Blancher

China's integration with the global economy is reflected in its rapidly growing role in international trade. China's exports and imports have grown faster than world trade for more than 20 years. While dramatic, thus far this is not an unprecedented event and is similar in magnitude to the surges in trade associated with earlier integration of other rapidly developing economies into the global trading system. As China's trade with the rest of the world has deepened, the composition and geographical pattern of its trade have also shifted. The share of imports by industrial economies accounted for by China has increased and exports to these markets have become more diversified. China has also become increasingly important within the Asian regional economy. Vertical specialization of production within Asia has led to an increasing share of China's imports coming from within the region. This, together with increasing imports for domestic consumption, has made China among the most important export destinations for other Asian countries.

Trade reforms and commitments made as part of the World Trade Organization (WTO) accession agreement have been crucial in promoting China's integration with the global trading system. These reforms, which took place over a 15-year period, have included substantial tariff reductions and the dismantling of most nontariff barriers (NTBs). Improved market access following WTO accession has also been important. While continued implementation of WTO commitments in the coming years will further facilitate China's ongoing integration with the global economy, it may also pose significant challenges for the authorities. Moreover, the extensive safeguards provisions under the WTO agreement represent a downside risk that could constrain China's export growth in the future.

China's Impact on Trade Patterns

Increasing Role in World Trade

China's international trade has expanded steadily since the opening of the economy in 1979. This

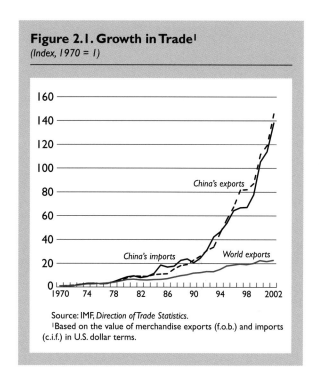

Figure 2.1. Growth in Trade[1]
(Index, 1970 = 1)

Source: IMF, *Direction of Trade Statistics.*
[1]Based on the value of merchandise exports (f.o.b.) and imports (c.i.f.) in U.S. dollar terms.

process began relatively slowly in the 1980s after the relaxation of pervasive and complex import and export controls, but accelerated in the 1990s with broader trade reforms, including significant tariff reductions. Both imports and exports have increased rapidly, and China's share in world trade has grown steadily since 1979 (Figure 2.1).[1] China has also increased its penetration into advanced country markets, and has simultaneously become a more important export destination, especially for regional economies (Tables 2.1 and 2.2). While the share of developed country imports accounted for by China has risen over the last two decades, China's role in

---

[1]China's trade is measured by merchandise exports (f.o.b.) and imports (c.i.f.) as reported by China's statistical authorities. Hong Kong SAR is treated as a separate customs territory unless otherwise noted.

Table 2.1. Market Share in Major Export Markets
(Imports from China divided by total imports, in percent)

	1970	1980	1990	1995	2000	2002	2003
Japan	1.4	3.1	5.1	10.7	14.5	18.3	18.5
United States	0.0	0.5	3.2	6.3	8.6	11.1	12.5
European Union[1]	0.6	0.7	2.0	3.8	6.2	7.5	8.9

Source: IMF, *Direction of Trade Statistics.*
[1]Excluding intra-EU trade.

Asian regional trade has also become increasingly important. Imports from the region are growing rapidly, and China is now among the most important export destinations for other Asian economies (Figure 2.2 and Table 2.3).

While a landmark development with implications for both the global and regional economies, China's integration with the world economy thus far is not unprecedented in either its scope or speed. The earlier experiences of Japan and the newly industrialized economies of Asia (NIEs)[2] were similar in terms of their rate of growth of exports as well as with respect to their increasing share in world exports over an extended period. Measuring export growth in U.S. dollars at constant prices shows that Japan, Korea, some member countries of the Association of South-East Asian Nations (ASEAN), and other NIEs maintained double-digit export growth rates on average for about a 30-year period. In fact, China's

exports have grown at a *slower* rate than the earlier experiences of these countries (Figure 2.3). This historical evidence, together with the still substantial development potential of the country, suggests that China could maintain relatively strong export growth for a number of years going forward.

Looking at the extent of penetration of key industrial country markets yields similar results. Using the U.S. market as an example, China currently accounts for 12 percent of U.S. imports compared with 9 percent for Japan and 3 percent for Korea. However, both Japan and Korea accounted for larger shares of U.S. imports in the past with Japan's share increasing steadily in the 1960s and 1970s, peaking at 22 percent in 1986. While Korea had the fastest export growth rate sustained over a 35-year period, because of its smaller size (relative to China and Japan), its import penetration of the U.S. market was not as pronounced. Still, Korea's share of U.S. imports reached 4½ percent in the late 1980s before declining slightly in recent years.

The extent of penetration of the U.S. import market can also be seen by looking at U.S. imports at the

_____
[2]Hong Kong SAR, Korea, Singapore, and Taiwan Province of China.

Table 2.2. Sources of Imports
(As a percent of China's total imports)

	1980	1990	1995	2000	2002	2003
Asia	15.0	41.0	47.1	53.5	53.1	52.8
ASEAN	3.4	5.6	7.4	9.3	10.4	11.3
Japan	26.5	14.2	21.9	17.8	18.1	18.0
Korea	...	0.4	7.8	10.0	9.7	10.4
Taiwan Province of China	...	...	11.2	11.3	12.9	12.9
European Union	15.8	17.0	16.1	13.3	13.1	12.9
United States	19.6	12.2	12.2	9.6	9.2	8.2

Sources: IMF, *Direction of Trade Statistics;* and CEIC database.

Figure 2.2. China's Trade with the Region[1]
(In percent)

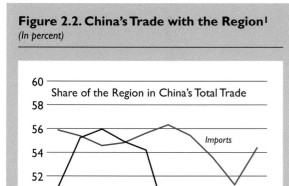

Share of the Region in China's Total Trade

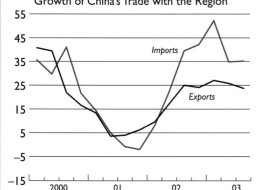

Growth of China's Trade with the Region

Source: CEIC database.
[1]Region comprises Hong Kong SAR, Indonesia, Japan, Korea, Malaysia, the Philippines, Singapore, and Taiwan Province of China.

Standard International Trade Classification (SITC) 2-digit level, where the number of product categories in which China had more than a 10 percent share of U.S. imports increased from 5 in 1990 to 16 in 2002. However, during the earlier periods, Japan's penetration of the U.S. market was even more pronounced, while Korea's was somewhat less. In 1962, Japan accounted for more than 10 percent of U.S. imports in 23 product categories at the 2-digit level and this level of import penetration was largely maintained throughout the 1970s before beginning a gradual decline to only 8 product categories in 2002. For Korea, the number of product categories that accounted for more than 10 percent of U.S. imports increased from 0 in the 1960s to 4 in the 1970s and

1980s before declining again to only 1 product category by 2002.

Changes in the Composition of Trade

China's export base has become diversified from an initial heavy reliance on textiles and other light manufacturing. In the early 1990s, light manufacturing accounted for more than 40 percent of China's exports. These products largely consisted of footwear, clothing, toys, and other miscellaneous manufactured articles. A large part of the remaining exports was accounted for by manufactured goods (mostly textiles) and machinery and transport (small electronics). In recent years, China has made substantial gains in other export categories, including more sophisticated electronics (office machines and automated data processing equipment, telecommunications and sound equipment, and electrical machinery), furniture, travel goods, and industrial supplies. For example, the proportion of China's exports represented by machinery and transport (which includes electronics) increased from 17 percent in 1993 to 41 percent in 2003, while the share of miscellaneous manufacturing declined from 42 percent to 28 percent.

Statistical indicators of dispersion illustrate an increase in overall export diversification. Detailed data on China's exports at the 2-digit SITC level are available only from 1994. The Herfindahl index and the coefficient of variation (which measure changes in the dispersion of export shares across categories) both indicate a significant increase in diversification between 1994 and 2000, while there was little change or even a marginal reversal during 2000–02 (Table 2.4). More extensive information available from detailed U.S. import data is also consistent with increased diversification of exports based on changes in the share of U.S. imports accounted for by China. These data also show a significant increase in diversification between 1990 and 2000 at both the 2-digit and 3-digit levels (Table 2.5).

The composition of imports reflects a high degree of vertical specialization of production within the Asia region. This can be seen from several indicators. First, a high share of imports for processing is embodied in China's exports. The ratio of imports for processing to total imports increased from about 35 percent of all imports in the early 1990s to about 50 percent by 1997 and has remained at about that level since. Similarly, imports for processing are estimated to be embodied in over 40 percent of China's exports. The impact of increased vertical specialization can be clearly seen in the rapid increase in imports of electronic integrated circuits and microassemblies—key components used in the assembly of electronic products (Figure 2.4). Sec-

Table 2.3. Exports of Selected Economies to China
(In percent of their total exports)

	1980	1985	1990	1995	2000	2002	2003
Japan	3.9	7.1	2.1	5.0	6.3	9.6	13.6
Korea	0.0	0.0	0.0	7.0	10.7	14.7	20.5
Hong Kong SAR	6.3	26.0	24.8	33.3	34.5	39.3	42.7
Singapore	1.6	1.5	1.5	2.3	3.9	5.5	7.0
Indonesia	0.0	0.5	3.2	3.8	4.5	5.1	7.4
Malaysia	1.7	1.0	2.1	2.6	3.1	5.6	10.8
Philippines	0.8	1.8	0.8	1.2	1.7	3.9	12.0
Thailand	1.9	3.8	1.2	2.9	4.1	5.2	7.1
India	0.3	0.3	0.1	0.9	1.8	4.2	6.4
European Union[1]	0.8	1.8	1.2	2.2	2.7	3.4	4.2
United States	1.7	1.8	1.2	2.0	2.1	3.2	3.9
Germany	0.6	1.2	0.6	1.5	1.6	2.2	2.6

Source: IMF, *Direction of Trade Statistics.*
[1]Adjusted for intra-EU trade.

ond, strong FDI inflows in China have come increasingly from countries in the region, especially the NIEs. During 2000–2002, NIEs plus Japan accounted for about 60 percent of the FDI in China, with the United States and Europe accounting for about 20 percent. Finally, the pattern of trade has changed substantially with increasing imports from Asia and a corresponding increase in exports going to developed economies, largely the United States and Europe.

Changes in Regional Trade

China's trade has been growing rapidly, with imports from nearly all trading partners growing at double-digit rates. Over the last two years (2002–2003), imports from Asia in U.S. dollar terms have increased at an average annual rate of 36 percent, while imports from Europe and the United States increased by average rates of 20 percent and 14 percent, respectively. On the export side, the average growth rates to industrial economies have been greater than within the region; exports to the United

Figure 2.3. Exports of Selected Economies[1]
(Index, beginning of period = 1; log scale)

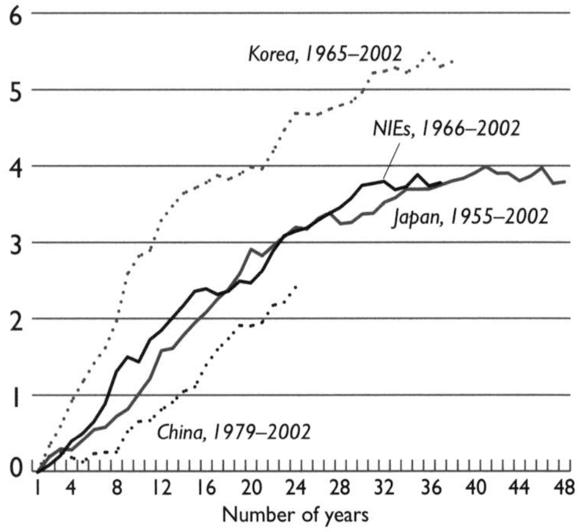

Source: IMF, *Direction of Trade Statistics.*
[1]Annual exports in U.S. dollars deflated by the U.S. GDP deflator. Newly industrialized economies include Hong Kong SAR, Korea, Singapore, and Taiwan Province of China.

Table 2.4. Indicators of Export Dispersion
(Share of total exports by SITC 2-digit)[1]

	1994	2000	2002
Coefficient of variation[2]	1.91	1.72	1.79
Herfindahl index[3]	0.073	0.062	0.066

Sources: CEIC; and IMF staff estimates.
[1]A lower number indicates more diversification (i.e., less dispersion in shares of each category in total exports).
[2]Coefficient of variation (standard deviation relative to sample mean).
[3]Herfindahl index (sum of squared export shares).

Table 2.5. Measures of Dispersion of Exports to the United States[1]
(Based on share of U.S. imports by SITC classification)

	1990	1995	2000	2002
SITC 1-digit				
CV[2]	1.39	1.57	1.38	1.32
H[3]	0.42	0.42	0.38	0.37
SITC 2-digit				
CV	1.88	1.86	1.70	1.61
H	0.12	0.11	0.09	0.09
SITC 3-digit				
Category 6				
CV	1.48	1.32	1.15	1.15
H	0.08	0.07	0.06	0.07
Category 7				
CV	2.00	1.50	1.41	1.23
H	0.12	0.08	0.09	0.10
Category 8				
CV	1.10	1.06	1.05	0.95
H	0.13	0.13	0.13	0.12
Total 6, 7, 8				
CV	1.61	1.48	1.30	1.20
H	0.07	0.06	0.05	0.05

Sources: CEIC and World Integrated Trade Solution databases.
[1]A lower number indicates more diversification (i.e., less dispersion in shares of each category in total exports). Categories 6, 7, and 8 refer to basic manufacturing, machinery and transportation, and miscellaneous manufacturing, respectively.
[2]Coefficient of variation (standard deviation relative to sample mean).
[3]Herfindahl index (sum of squared export shares).

Figure 2.4. Trade in Electronic Products: Monthly Imports of Electronic Components
(In millions of U.S. dollars; three-month moving average)

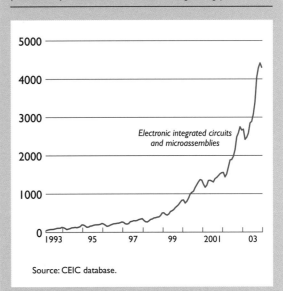

Electronic integrated circuits and microassemblies

Source: CEIC database.

tinued to increase, producing a decline in China's overall trade surplus, to $25 billion, compared with $30 billion in 2002 (Table 2.6). Adjusting for the large volume of China's trade that transits through Hong Kong SAR does not change this basic conclusion.[3]

WTO Accession: Commitments, Opportunities, and Risks

China's Commitments and Compliance

The tariff reductions planned by China in the context of its WTO accession are largely the continuation of a long-standing trend. This trend is reflected in the decreasing level and dispersion of tariffs and the continued reduction in NTBs, especially since the early 1990s (Table 2.7). Past reforms also introduced widespread import tariff exemptions, especially for processing trade and foreign investment and, therefore, a

States and Europe grew at an annual rate of 31 percent and 33 percent, respectively, and exports to Asia by 26 percent. While processing trade is an important contributor to the growth in imports from the region, imports for domestic consumption are also increasing rapidly. As a result, China's imports from other parts of the world are increasing dramatically. For example, in 2003, imports increased by 81 percent from Latin America and 54 percent from Africa, and China is now the third largest importer of developing country exports after the United States and the European Union.

While China's overall trade balance did not change significantly during 2001-2003, these changes in regional trade patterns caused a significant shift in bilateral trade balances. China's trade surplus with the United States and the European Union increased significantly from 1997 to 2002, but this was offset by an increasing trade deficit with the rest of Asia. These trends continued in 2003 as the deficits with Asian countries con-

---

[3]The role of Hong Kong SAR in China's trade is the primary explanation for the discrepancy in official trade statistics between China and the United States. China's customs statistics show a trade surplus with the United States in 2002 of $43 billion. Taking into account statistics from Hong Kong SAR on imports from the mainland that are reexported to the United States, and imports from the United States that are reexported to China produces an adjusted estimate of $74 billion.

Table 2.6. China's Bilateral Trade Balances with Selected Economies
(In billions of U.S. dollars)

	China plus Hong Kong SAR[1]			China		
	1997	2002	2003	1997	2002	2003
United States	41	74	88	16	43	55
European Union	9	18	29	5	10	18
Japan	14	−18	−30	3	−5	−14
Korea	−12	−19	−30	−6	−13	−21
Taiwan Province of China	−24	−42	−51	−13	−31	−37
Hong Kong SAR	...	...	...	37	48	61
ASEAN	−10	−18	−30	0	−8	−15
Others	6	−7	−11	−1	−13	−22
Total	−4	−12	−35	40	30	25

Source: CEIC database.

[1]By taking mainland China and Hong Kong SAR together, this measure includes imports and exports to the mainland that are intermediated through Hong Kong SAR. During 2002–2003, Hong Kong SAR intermediated about 22 percent of the mainland's trade.

majority of China's imports were in effect not subject to any tariffs in 2000. Under its WTO commitments, China will further reduce its average tariff rate to 10 percent by 2005 (Box 2.1). Overall, under the WTO

Table 2.7. Tariffs

	Unweighted Average[1]	Weighted Average[1]	Dispersion (SD)	Max
1982	55.6	...	...	...
1985	43.3	...	...	...
1988	43.7	...	...	...
1991	44.1	...	...	...
1992	42.9	40.6	...	220.0
1993	39.9	38.4	29.9	220.0
1994	36.3	35.5	27.9	...
1995	35.2	26.8	...	220.0
1996	23.6	22.6	17.4	121.6
1997	17.6	16.0	13.0	121.6
1998	17.5	15.7	13.0	121.6
2000	16.4	...	...	...
2001	15.3	9.1	12.1	121.6
2002	12.3	6.4	9.1	71.0

Sources: Chinese authorities; United Nations Conference on Trade and Development; World Bank; WTO; and IMF staff estimates

[1]The unweighted average is based on a simple average of the statutory rates for the relevant year. The weighted average is based on the statutory rates weighted by the value of imports in each category.

agreement, its trade regime will be increasingly tariff-based and more transparent.

In contrast with the continuity in tariff reductions, China's recent commitments on trade in services and other trade-related activities represent milestones.[4] Plans include the opening of key services sectors where foreign participation was previously nonexistent or marginal, notably telecommunications, financial services, and insurance. In those sectors, full access will eventually be guaranteed to foreign providers through transparent and automatic licensing procedures. China will also remove restrictions on trading and domestic distribution for most products. Apart from market access, China made major commitments on trade-related activities, such as national treatment and nondiscrimination principles, and with respect to Trade-Related Investment Measures (TRIMs) and Trade-Related Aspects of Intellectual Property Rights (TRIPs). Compliance with such commitments is likely to have far-reaching implications domestically, including by encouraging greater internal integration of domestic markets (through the removal of inter-provincial barriers). Moreover, the commitment to comply with the principles and rules of the international trading system will improve the transparency of the domestic policy environment.

A special WTO procedure, the Transitional Review Mechanism, was established as part of China's

[4]Indeed, some observers have argued that they represent the most radical services reform program negotiated in the WTO to date (Lardy, 2002; and Mattoo, 2002).

Box 2.1. Selected Aspects of China's WTO Accession[1]

Trade in Goods

All tariffs on imported goods are to be eliminated or reduced, mostly by 2004. Tariffs on industrial goods will be reduced to an average of 9 percent, and import quotas will be removed by 2005. Tariffs on agricultural goods will be lowered to an average of 15 percent.

Trade in Services

Foreign access is to be ensured through transparent and automatic licensing procedures in various sectors, including banking and insurance, legal and other professional services, telecommunications, and tourism. Specifically:

- *Right to trade and distribution.* Within two years foreign service suppliers will be permitted to engage in the retailing of all products (implemented at end-2003); within three years (by end-2004) all firms will have the right to import and export all goods except those subject to state trading monopolies (e.g., oil and fertilizers); within five years (by end-2006), foreign firms will be allowed to distribute virtually all goods domestically.
- *Banking.* Foreign financial institutions were permitted to provide services without client restrictions for foreign currency business upon accession; local currency services to Chinese companies within two years (implemented at end-2003); and services to all Chinese clients within five years (by end-2006).

Trading and Investment Regimes

- *National treatment/nondiscrimination.* Measures and practices that discriminate against imported products or foreign companies will be removed.
- *Export subsidies.* Upon accession, all forms of export subsidies inconsistent with WTO rules, including grants and tax breaks linked to export performance, were eliminated.
- *Trade-Related Investment Measures (TRIMs).* Foreign investment approvals will no longer be subject to mandatory requirements (e.g., technology transfer or local content requirements).
- *Trade-Related Aspects of Intellectual Property Rights (TRIPs).* China will enforce the rights protecting intellectual property within China.
- *Agricultural subsidies.* China has agreed to limit domestic agricultural subsidies to 8.5 percent of the value of production (i.e., less than the 10 percent limit allowed for developing countries under the WTO Agreement on Agriculture), and to eliminate all agricultural export subsidies upon accession.

Trading Partner Safeguards

- *Transitional product-specific safeguard mechanism.* As provided under the WTO Agreement on Safeguards, a country may impose restrictions on imports if it can demonstrate that they cause or threaten to cause serious injury to domestic firms producing similar products.
- *Special safeguard mechanism for China's textile and clothing exports.*
- *Antidumping.* Under the WTO agreement, other members can invoke "nonmarket economy" provisions to determine dumping cases for 15 years following accession. Nonmarket economy provisions imply that domestic prices cannot be used as a reference point and make it much easier to reach a positive finding in an antidumping investigation.

---

[1]A more complete description of the terms of China's WTO accession is available at http://www.wto.org/english/news_e/pres01_e/pr252_e.htm.

Protocol of Accession. It requires that China's compliance be reviewed by the WTO on an annual basis in the early years. The 2002 and 2003 reviews did not reveal any major source of contention with regard to China's implementation of its WTO commitments, and a widely shared assessment seems to be that specific difficulties reflect primarily technical problems instead of a broad pattern of noncompliance.[5] Looking ahead, China's compliance with agreed commitments will be continually tested, as it requires adequate enforcement of new rules, including at the provincial and municipal levels, where vested interests and capacity constraints may hamper progress.

---

[5]See, for example, United States Trade Representative (2002).

Market Access Prospects

Increased market access overseas is the most immediate benefit from WTO accession for China. China was permanently granted most-favored-nation (MFN) treatment by other WTO members, a significant step toward normalizing its trade relations. Upon accession, several trading partners eliminated many of their restrictions on imports from China. Over time, easier access to foreign markets is likely to boost China's exports in a number of sectors. In the case of textiles and clothing, for example, WTO accession implies that China has formally been included in the Uruguay Round Agreement on Textiles and Clothing (ATC) and, like other ATC members, will eventually obtain unrestricted access to textile and clothing export markets. China's world

---

Box 2.2. The International Impact of China's WTO Accession

Methodologies. Research aimed at quantifying the impact of China's WTO accession intensified in the late 1990s. It has focused on the specific impact of WTO-related trade reforms in China against baseline projections incorporating Uruguay Round trade reforms. The welfare impact has been assessed based on global general equilibrium models: the Global Trade Analysis Project (GTAP) developed at Purdue University, which focuses on terms of trade and trade flow effects, is one of these models; other studies are based on the G-Cubed Asia Pacific Model developed at the Australian National University.

Results. Most studies concur that China's WTO accession will entail an overall welfare gain for China and the world as a whole. However, since China's tariffs have already been lowered substantially, this effect is not likely to be sizable in the future. Another general result is that countries will tend to benefit (or lose) in proportion to the degree of complementarity between their trade patterns and China's. More detailed results include the following:[1]

- Sustaining China's growth momentum should provide benefits to most of its trading partners: in addition to the prominent role played by processing trade, imports for domestic use have increased rapidly and outbound tourism grew by 37 percent in 2002. Multinational companies are increasingly investing in China to meet local final demand rather than solely for reexport purposes. China's energy and mineral imports are also expected to continue to increase rapidly, providing benefits to resource-rich countries. These developments have contributed to maintaining strong growth in the Asian region despite low growth in the rest of the world.

- The NIEs of Asia, in particular, would gain from China's expanding trade: most of them have a complementary trade pattern with China and are benefiting from processing trade, as reflected in the rapid increase in their exports of intermediate products and components to China. However, China's exports are moving up the value-added chain and domestic production of components is rising. While China could pose a more direct competitive threat to these economies in the future, the benefits from growing intraindustry trade are likely to dominate.

- ASEAN countries and South Asia are also experiencing benefits as exports of all countries to China are expanding rapidly. However, to the extent that there is competition in the export of labor-intensive products, some of these economies may have to undergo significant adjustments. For example, the expected future growth in China's clothing exports could have an adverse impact, especially for quota-dependent low- and middle-income economies—although this impact could be mitigated for some countries by increased opportunities for textile exports to China as inputs for China's clothing exports. ASEAN countries may also have to adjust to a greater share of FDI in the region going to China, and take steps to ensure that technological innovations and productivity improvements continue to take place in their economies.

Limits to existing research. The actual impact of China's WTO accession on the rest of the world may prove greater than such analyses would suggest. First, most existing models have several technical limitations, including uncertainties in estimated trade elasticities stemming from rapid changes in the structure of China's and the region's international trade. More fundamentally, most models fail to take into account key aspects of China's WTO membership, such as the opening of trade in services or reforms that will remove obstacles to foreign investment and further change China's role as a global export base.

---

[1]See, for example, Adhikari and Yang (2002), Hertel and Walmsley (2000), Ianchovichina and Martin (2003), and Panitchpakdi and Clifford (2002). For the impact on developing countries, see Yang (2003).

---

export market share in this sector could then surge significantly.[6] China will also benefit from the treatment of future trade conflicts within the multilateral dispute settlement procedures under the WTO. However, China's accession protocol also incorporates provisions that could constrain China's export market gains in the early years. While such provisions reflect WTO principles, they are widely seen in the case of China as going beyond usual practice in recent WTO accession cases.[7]

Potential Implications of China's Role in World Trade

While China will benefit from its WTO accession, especially through efficiency gains and direct bene-

---

[6]The recent increase in China's footwear exports (which are not subject to quota restrictions) provides an indication in this regard: while China's world export market shares in textile and clothing products remained at about 15 percent from 1990 to 2002, its market share in footwear increased from 7.3 percent in 1990 to 28.4 percent in 2000.

[7]See, for example, Lardy (2002), pp. 80–89.

fits for Chinese consumers, the world economy will also gain from China's transformation into a leading international importer of both industrial and consumer goods. Key steps in this regard are China's decisions to open sectors that are crucial to its partners and to substantially improve its business environment. In the Asian region, the benefits associated with further trade specialization, as well as China's own increased domestic consumption, are substantial. Indeed, these trends have already contributed to support sustained trade and growth in the region despite slow growth in the rest of the world.

Empirical analyses predict moderate welfare gains for the world economy and a net impact on individual countries that would depend on the degree of complementarity between their trade patterns and China's (Box 2.2). In particular, Asian economies that have a complementary trade pattern with China, including the NIEs, are benefiting from processing trade. However, since China's exports are moving up the value-added chain, China could pose a more direct competitive threat even to these economies in the future. Also, some ASEAN countries and South Asia may have to undergo some adjustment to the extent that they compete with China in the export of labor-intensive products. Asian economies may also have to adjust to a greater share of FDI in the region going to China, and will need to take steps to sustain technological innovations and productivity improvements.

Individual countries can maximize their gains from China's emergence and minimize the associated costs by increasing the flexibility of their economies through structural reforms. A successful response to China's emergence will involve significant intersectoral mobility. As resources move to more productive areas, transitional problems may arise, particularly for less-skilled workers. Affected countries would do best to speed up their own liberalization and integration, which will improve resource allocation and allow them to better pursue their own comparative advantage. For advanced countries, this will likely entail shifting factors of production to skill- and capital-intensive activities.

For middle-income developing countries with relatively well educated workforces, enhanced labor flexibility, together with efforts to upgrade human capital through education and training, will help them move up the value-added chain. Countries with a relatively large pool of less-skilled workers will face a more difficult task, but they will need to speed up reforms to create employment opportunities for less-skilled workers and increase investment in workers' training and skill upgrading. Broader trade liberalization, especially by the advanced countries, could significantly aid this process by removing constraints on these countries' exports.

Beyond the impact on individual countries, the expansion of China's role in international trade raises several challenges. There may be a greater risk of trade disputes and retaliatory measures as a result of the use of the extensive safeguards procedures with potentially negative impacts on international trade volumes. There are also risks on the domestic front, as growth sustainability could be threatened by the impact of WTO-related reforms on the agricultural sector and rural income, on SOE and financial sector losses, and on various vested interests, especially at the provincial level.

However, WTO accession will likely mitigate some of these risks and help ensure that the benefits of China's emergence in world trade are distributed broadly. Since China can be expected to maintain strong export growth for a number of years going forward, the steps it has taken as part of its WTO accession to open its own markets are especially important. For example, and as noted above, the benefits to the Asian region are already substantial as China has become a major export destination for other Asian countries, and is increasingly importing from other regions of the world as well. That this process is taking place within global rules defined in a multilateral context rather than through regional or bilateral trade arrangements should help to ensure that the benefits of China's increasing integration into the world trading system are spread more broadly throughout the global economy.

III Price Dynamics in China

Tarhan Feyzioğlu

Between the mid-1990s and 2003, China had an average annual inflation rate of only about 1 percent, with periods of mild deflation, even though output growth was very strong, averaging more than 8 percent a year (Figure 3.1). Moreover, price increases were minimal despite the accommodative stances of fiscal and monetary policies. This section analyzes the key factors that have led to low inflation or deflation in this high-growth environment. The econometric results suggest that declining commodity prices and tariff cuts exerted significant downward pressures on inflation in China, while demand factors played a smaller role.

Stylized Facts

After a period of sharp price increases, peaking at 27 percent in late 1994, inflation declined rapidly and, by early 1998, China entered into its first episode of deflation (Figure 3.2). Deflation lasted for around two years, with price declines averaging around 1 percent and the largest decline at 2.2 percent in April–May 1999.[1] In early 2000, mild inflation emerged, but it was short lived. The largest price increase registered during this period was 1.7 percent (May 2001). Deflation reemerged in late 2001 and lasted for more than a year. Since the beginning of 2003, China has been experiencing low inflation, which reached 3.2 percent (year-on-year) by end-2003.

In examining price changes at a disaggregated level, one pattern stands out: prices of tradable consumption goods declined persistently between 1997 and 2002 (Figure 3.3). In particular, prices of clothing and housing appliances (which have an estimated weight of 14 percent in the aggregate consumer price index (CPI)) declined by a cumulative 8 percent during 1998–2002, and food prices (which have an esti-

Figure 3.1. Real GDP Growth and CPI Inflation
(Annual percent change)

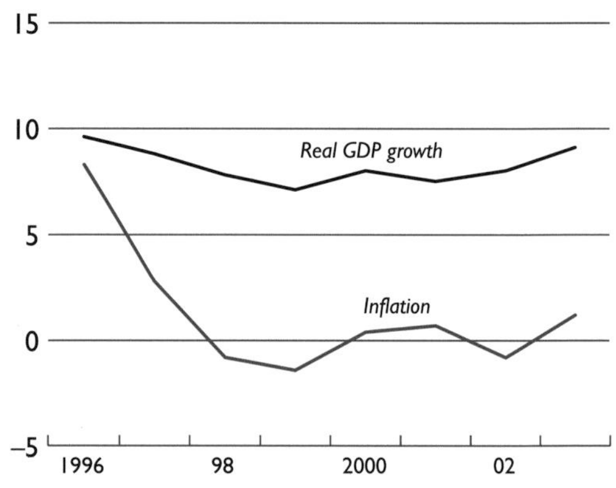

Source: CEIC database.

mated weight of 35 percent) by a cumulative 10 percent during 1997–2000.[2] Starting in late 2002, however, food and energy prices started to increase, and through 2003, tradable goods' prices have been increasing at a moderate pace.

Prices of nontradables, on the other hand, increased significantly until 2001. In particular, service prices increased, on average, by 12 percent during 1998–2000. Starting in mid-2001, however, prices of most services began to decline (e.g., medical care) or ceased to increase (e.g., housing). This slowdown seems to have come to an end by late 2002, and prices of most services, including housing,

---

[1]All growth rates are year-on-year changes. Seasonally adjusted monthly changes could indicate earlier turning points; however, data limitations—in particular, breaks in the series—do not allow proper seasonal adjustment.

[2]The weights are the estimated coefficients from a least squares regression, where the dependent variable is CPI growth and the explanatory variables are the growth rates of its components. Official data on the weights of the components of the CPI basket are not publicly available.

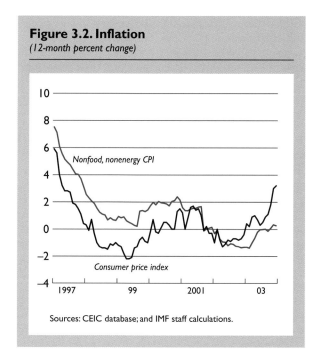

Figure 3.2. Inflation
(12-month percent change)

Sources: CEIC database; and IMF staff calculations.

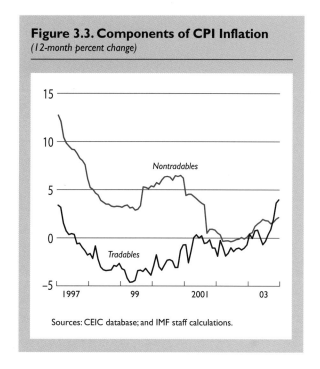

Figure 3.3. Components of CPI Inflation
(12-month percent change)

Sources: CEIC database; and IMF staff calculations.

have started to pick up in early 2003. These price developments indicate that, while the first deflationary episode was the result of strong price declines in the tradable goods sectors, weaker service prices were important in the emergence of the second deflationary episode.

While most prices in China are now determined by market forces, the remaining price controls still play a role in aggregate price dynamics. Most price controls were abolished by 1993, but pharmaceutical prices and prices for health care and education are still administratively determined. Most controls are in the form of "guidelines" issued by the State Development and Reform Commission, and are ceilings for prices and fees. The weights of these components in the aggregate CPI are estimated to be around 10–15 percent. There are indications that price increases in these sectors were kept at moderate levels because of concerns about social stability (rising unemployment associated with state-owned enterprise (SOE) reforms and reforms in the agriculture sector), particularly in recent years, when these concerns have intensified.

Potential measurement problems, especially in service sector prices, suggest that changes in the aggregate CPI should be interpreted with caution. While the administered prices in health care and education have not increased significantly, there are indications that prices of similar services provided by nonstate entities have been increasing markedly. Also, the housing price index could be underestimating the actual services received from housing,

because the index is linked to government-controlled housing units, which do not reflect actual rental price increases in the market. In addition, the imputed rent is linked to the interest rate and falls as interest rates decline, as was the case in 2002. Nevertheless, the total weight of these components is not large enough to play a significant role in the changes in the aggregate index.

Other measures of aggregate prices show similar movements as in the CPI (Figure 3.4). For example, the retail sales price index, which covers most of the prices that are included in the CPI, but excludes services and includes small retail items that might also be used for investment purposes, moves in parallel to the CPI index. During the sample period, changes in this index remained consistently below changes in the CPI index, reflecting the fact that inflation in services was higher than inflation in other prices. Inflation based on the producer price index also does not deviate from CPI inflation for long periods, although it is more volatile. Moreover, it leads CPI inflation in the sense that it switches direction several months before CPI inflation does.

Key Sources of Price Changes

Both demand and supply factors could potentially account for changes in prices. On the supply side, labor productivity in China has been increasing rapidly as a result of strong investment rates, which averaged 40 percent of GDP in the last 10 years.

Figure 3.4. Alternative Measures of Inflation
(12-month percent change)

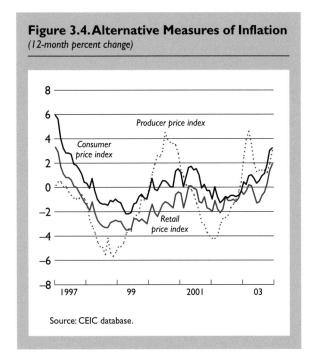

Source: CEIC database.

High investment rates have been supported by a high domestic saving rate and strong foreign direct investment (FDI), which averaged more than $35 billion annually during this period. Competition in domestic markets has intensified, as China has been lowering trade barriers and opening up its markets to foreign competition for many years. This process has been spurred further by China's WTO accession in December 2001 (see Lardy, 2002; and Section II). In addition, monopolies are in the process of being broken up, and SOE reform is allowing the private sector to increase its share in the economy.

There have also been changes in external and domestic demand. External demand was weak during the Asian crisis, which intensified the downward pressures on prices, not only because of a slowdown in overall economic activity, but also through diversion of some export goods to local markets. On the domestic side, the relatively slow growth of income in rural areas may also have contributed to lower overall prices. On the other hand, macroeconomic policies were accommodative during most of this period, helping to stimulate demand and prop up prices. In particular, the fiscal deficit widened from less than 1 percent of GDP (official definition) in 1996 to 3 percent of GDP in 2002. Monetary policy was also accommodative, especially in the last few years.

Other more transitory factors may also have had a significant impact on inflation in China. World nonfuel commodity prices declined significantly during both deflationary episodes.[3] In particular, the world nonfuel commodity index declined by 23 percent (year-on-year) by August 1998, started to recover in early 1999, peaked in late 2000, and then started to decline again. Import tariffs have also been reduced significantly in recent years, with the average tariff rate (unweighted) declining from 23.6 percent in 1996 to 11 percent in 2003 (see Section II). Such a decline would have a direct impact on consumer prices, as well as an indirect effect through lower costs of imports of intermediate goods and other inputs. Moreover, exchange rate changes may have had some impact. Although the renminbi has been closely tied to the U.S. dollar since 1994, China's nominal effective exchange rate has fluctuated significantly, registering a cumulative appreciation of 35 percent between 1994 and early 2002. Between then and end-2003, the nominal effective exchange rate depreciated by 15 percent.

Regression Results

To capture the potential impact of these factors on price dynamics in China, the following regression was estimated in linear form using quarterly data for the period 1996–2003:[4]

$$inf_t = f(\text{lagged } inf,\ prod_t,\ ygap_t,\ g_t,\\ M2_{t-1},\ comm_t,\ tariff_t,\ neer_t)$$

where *inf* is CPI inflation; *prod* is productivity growth in the whole economy; *ygap* is the output gap, calculated as the deviations from trend output obtained using the Hodrick-Prescott filter; *g* is the quarterly fiscal balance as a ratio to output; *M2* is the rate of growth of broad money; *comm* is the change in the world nonfuel commodity price index; *tariff* is the change in the average tariff rate; and *neer* is the change in the nominal effective exchange rate (Figure 3.5).[5]

The model assumes that broad money growth affects price changes with a lag; therefore, several lag values of this variable are used in the regression.[6]

---

[3]The index used in this analysis is the overall index aggregated using global weights.

[4]The sample is truncated at 1996 because prior data cover China's high-inflation period, for which only partial data are available on a quarterly basis. Moreover, only partially appending this high-inflation period to the low-inflation period could potentially distort the estimates for the latter period, which is of more interest.

[5]All growth rates are year-on-year. See the appendix for a detailed description of the data sources and calculations.

[6]The use of domestic credit growth as an alternative variable to capture the impact of monetary developments on inflation did not fundamentally change the results. The correlation between M2 growth and credit growth over the period is about 50 percent.

Figure 3.5. Variables Used in the Regression

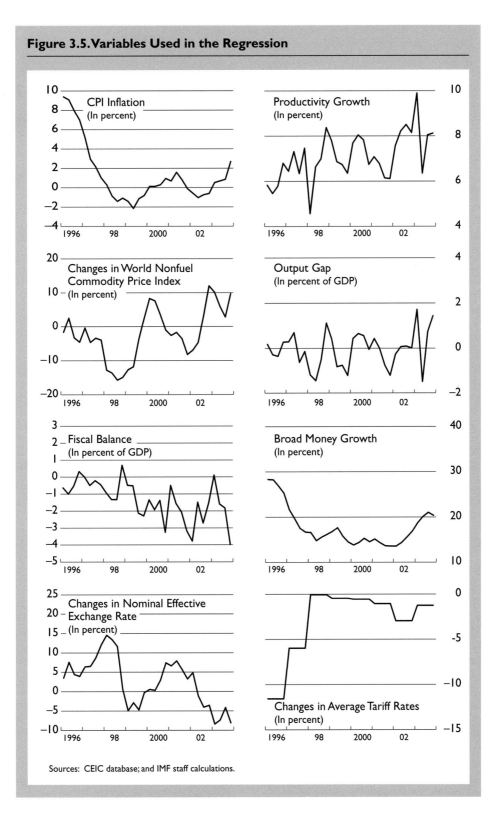

Sources: CEIC database; and IMF staff calculations.

It is also assumed that fiscal balances are not affected contemporaneously by inflation, because taxes are collected with a lag. Regarding the nonfuel com-

modity prices, China's increasing trade and demand for investment goods have boosted some specific commodity prices; however, given the relative size of the Chinese economy in the global economy (3–6 percent during the sample period), it is assumed that China does not have a significant impact on the overall commodity price index.

Inflation expectations are not modeled explicitly; however, the estimated coefficients could be considered as the reduced-form coefficients from a richer model that incorporates expectations. In that sense, the coefficients capture direct effects as well as indirect effects through expectation formation. A single equation approach was preferred to a structural vector autoregression (VAR) model commonly used in estimating the impact of demand and supply shocks on output and inflation, because a VAR model that is as rich and contains as many variables requires a longer time series than is available.

The model is estimated using ordinary least squares. First, a general model was estimated that included all the variables that could potentially affect inflation. Next, the variables and lags that were not statistically significant were eliminated sequentially, with the variable that has the lowest probability of having a significant coefficient eliminated first. The final result was not sensitive to the elimination sequence, since different elimination sequences produced similar results. A set of diagnostic tests on the final regression results did not indicate the presence of serial correlation in the error terms or significant break points.[7]

The results for the final specification are presented in Table 3.1. The results suggest strong persistence in CPI inflation, since the estimated coefficient on the lagged dependent variable is large (0.71), even though it is significantly smaller than one.[8] This also implies that the total impact of a shock to inflation is spread across two years, with two-thirds of the total impact observed within the first year.

Structural factors, in particular strong productivity growth and lower tariffs, appear to have been important determinants of inflation. The coefficient estimates suggest that a 1 percentage point increase in productivity growth would have lowered CPI inflation (or increased deflation) by more than 0.3 percentage point during the same quarter and, owing to the persistence in the inflation variable, inflation would have continued to decline in subsequent periods, but at a diminishing rate. Similarly, a 1 percentage point cut in the average tariff rate would have lowered inflationary pressures by close to 0.1 percentage point with a half-year lag.

---

[7]The tests included recursive coefficient estimates and CUSUM of squares test.

[8]Augmented Dickey-Fuller and Phillips-Perron tests rejected the null hypothesis of a unit root in the inflation rate. The large coefficient on the lagged dependent variable probably partly explains the high R-squared statistic.

Table 3.1. OLS Estimates of a Reduced-Form Inflation Equation[1]
(Dependent variable: four-quarter CPI inflation)

Variable	Coefficient (t-statistics)
Constant	0.50
	(0.41)
Lagged CPI inflation	0.71
	(22.15)
Productivity growth	−0.34
	(2.65)
Changes in average tariff rates, lagged twice	0.08
	(2.60)
Output gap as a percent of GDP	0.51
	(3.07)
Fiscal balance in percent of GDP	−0.09
	(1.87)
Broad money growth, lagged once	0.13
	(4.68)
Changes in the world commodity price index	0.05
	(6.75)
Number of observations	32
R-squared	0.98
Prob(F-statistic)	0.00

Source: IMF staff calculations.
[1]Sample period is Q1:1996–Q4:2003. The figures in parentheses are absolute t-statistics, based on standard errors calculated using Newey-West heteroscedasticity and autocorrelation consistent covariances (lag truncation = 3).

Demand-side factors also seem to have played a role in price formation during the sample period. The coefficient on the output gap variable is significant, and implies that a 1 percentage point increase in GDP growth above the trend would have increased inflation by 0.5 percentage point. Similarly, a 1 percentage point increase in growth of broad money would have resulted in a more than 0.1 percentage point increase in inflation. The coefficient on the fiscal balance is significant but small, and suggests that a 1 percent of GDP increase in the fiscal deficit would have increased inflation by less than 0.1 percentage point.

World nonfuel commodity prices also appear to affect inflation in China. The coefficient estimate implies that a 10 percent increase in the world nonfuel commodity price index would have increased the inflation rate by 0.5 percentage point. The nominal effective exchange rate, on the other hand, was not a significant determinant of inflation during the sample period. Its coefficient was consistently insignificant in various regression specifications (sometimes with the wrong sign), and this variable was dropped from the final equation.

Figure 3.6. First-Round Impact of the Regression Variables on Inflation[1]

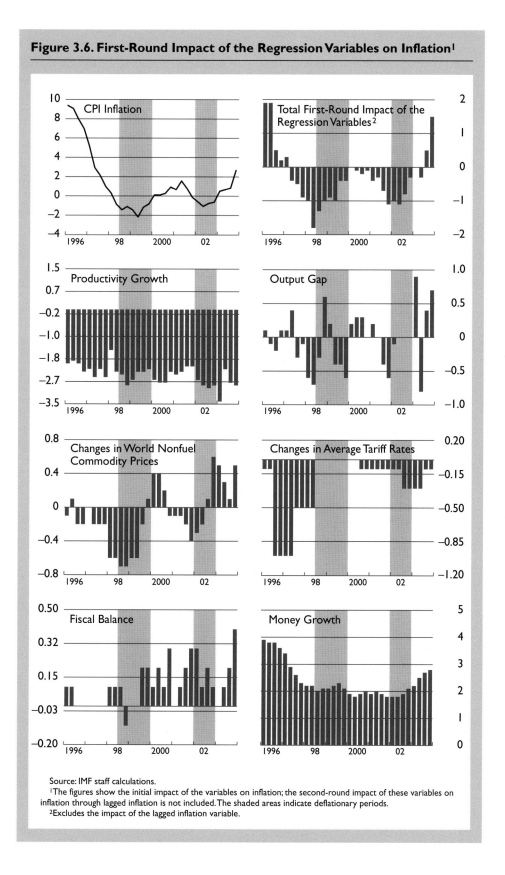

Source: IMF staff calculations.

[1]The figures show the initial impact of the variables on inflation; the second-round impact of these variables on inflation through lagged inflation is not included. The shaded areas indicate deflationary periods.

[2]Excludes the impact of the lagged inflation variable.

Observed movements of the explanatory variables, coupled with the coefficient estimates, suggest that structural factors and world commodity prices were key factors that led to both deflationary episodes (Figure 3.6). Prior to and at the beginning of the first deflationary episode, there were large reductions in tariff rates, exerting significant downward pressures on prices during this period. There were also further cuts in tariffs before and during the second deflationary episode. In addition, during these periods productivity growth remained high—in particular during the second deflationary episode—and commodity prices declined significantly, further increasing deflationary pressures. Demand factors also contributed, as the output gap remained negative, albeit small, during both deflationary periods.

Several of these factors were reversed in 2002–03, ending the second deflationary episode. Commodity prices in particular changed sharply, increasing around 20 percent during this period. In addition, demand factors picked up, especially in 2003 (except during the second quarter that reflected the SARS epidemic): output growth was significantly above trend, the fiscal deficit remained close to 3 percent of GDP, and money growth had picked up. Combined, these inflationary pressures were stronger than the downward price pressures from continued productivity growth, and led to a sharp increase of inflation by the end of 2003.

Appendix: Data Sources and Calculations

All data are year-on-year growth rates of quarterly data from the CEIC database, unless otherwise noted.

inf: the CPI inflation rate.

prod: aggregated differences of the output growth rates and the employment growth rates in the primary, secondary, and tertiary sectors. Quarterly employment figures are interpolated from annual sectoral employment data provided by the National Bureau of Statistics of China.

ygap: the deviation of quarterly output growth rates from the trend, which is obtained using the Hodrick-Prescott filter with smoothing parameter equal to 1600.

g: the ratio of the quarterly fiscal balance of the general government to quarterly GDP; seasonally adjusted using X-12.

M2: growth of broad money.

Comm: growth rate of the world commodity price index (source: IMF, Research Department).

Tariff: unweighted average tariff rates (source: Rumbaugh and Blancher, 2004).

Neer: trade-weighted index of the nominal exchange rates; bilateral exchange rates are provided by the IMF.

IV Exchange Rate Dynamics

Tao Wang

China's rapid export growth and accumulation of international reserves have generated considerable interest in analyzing the renminbi exchange rate. This section examines China's real exchange rate developments between 1980 and 2003 and the factors underlying these developments from three different angles. First, various measures of the real effective exchange rate are constructed to study its evolution over the past two decades. Second, results from different approaches to estimating equilibrium exchange rates are summarized. Reflecting the extreme difficulties of this exercise for a developing country, existing methodologies provide a wide range of estimates with a great deal of uncertainty attached to each of them. Finally, a structural vector autoregression approach is used to study the underlying forces driving real exchange rate variations. This analysis shows how the medium-term path of the exchange rate depends on the types of shocks hitting the economy.

Exchange Rate Developments: A Historical Overview

During much of the 1980s, China had a fixed exchange rate system although the renminbi was devalued frequently, reflecting economic developments and waves of opening up of the economy. Between 1988 and 1993, China had a dual exchange rate system where the official fixed exchange rate coexisted with the market-determined rate in the swap centers. The swap centers were established in 1988 as an expansion and centralization of the fragmented markets that had emerged since the early 1980s. In the swap centers, exporters, importers, and other parties with foreign exchange supply or needs could transact at a market-determined exchange rate. The swap market rate depreciated sharply in the early 1990s, while the fixed official rate became increasingly overvalued. In 1994, the official rate was devalued and unified with the exchange rate at the swap centers (which accounted for an estimated 80 percent of current account foreign exchange transactions at the time), and the exchange rate system was officially changed into a managed float.

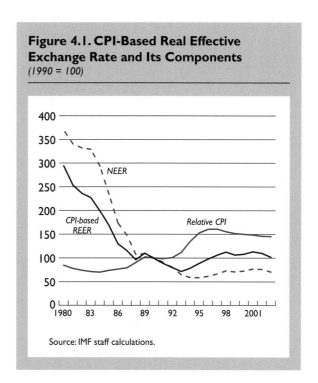

Figure 4.1. CPI-Based Real Effective Exchange Rate and Its Components
(1990 = 100)

Source: IMF staff calculations.

Since then, China has officially had a managed floating exchange rate system although the currency has been de facto fixed to the U.S. dollar since 1995.

Although China has had either a de jure or de facto fixed exchange rate regime over the past two decades, the real effective exchange rate (REER) based on the consumer price index (CPI) has experienced sharp swings.[1] Throughout the 1980s and early 1990s, the CPI-based REER depreciated drastically through large devaluations of the nominal exchange rate as China steadily abandoned its annual quantitative plans for foreign trade and opened up its economy (Figure 4.1). Subsequently, when the renminbi was more or less fixed to the U.S. dollar, the

---

[1]REER data are annual averages. For the period that a dual exchange rate system existed, the nominal exchange rate used in the calculation is a combination of both the official and swap center exchange rates, weighted by the transaction volumes.

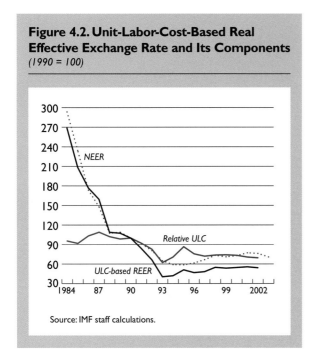

Figure 4.2. Unit-Labor-Cost-Based Real Effective Exchange Rate and Its Components
(1990 = 100)

Source: IMF staff calculations.

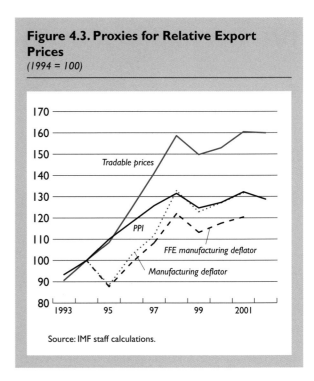

Figure 4.3. Proxies for Relative Export Prices
(1994 = 100)

Source: IMF staff calculations.

REER appreciated steadily until the onset of the Asian crisis in mid-1997, mainly reflecting the faster CPI growth in China than in partner countries.

Between mid-1997 and mid-1998, with the renminbi being held stable against the U.S. dollar, China's real effective exchange rate appreciated, mostly on account of the depreciation against the U.S. dollar of the Japanese yen and the currencies of the countries hit by the Asian crisis. This appreciation was soon reversed as Asian currencies rebounded and inflation in China was much lower than in its trading partners. Since 1999, China's CPI inflation has continued to be low relative to partner countries, and the modest appreciation of the nominal effective exchange rate until 2001 and the depreciation since then largely reflect the U.S. dollar's movements against other currencies. The average index for the CPI-based REER in 2003 is depreciated relative to its level in 1997 by roughly 4 percent.

Alternative measures of the REER show a similar trend. Figure 4.2 plots data on the real value of the renminbi based on relative unit labor costs (ULC) in the manufacturing sector. Between 1984 and 1993, the ULC-based REER depreciated by about 85 percent, much more sharply than the CPI-based REER, partly because wage growth generally fell short of the rise in labor productivity (with the exception of the period between 1985 and 1987). Between 1998 and 2002, wage growth has been in line with productivity and the ULC-based REER has been relatively stable. Figure 4.3 presents the producer price index (PPI)-based REER and measures of relative

export prices, and they have also risen since the mid-1990s, with much of the upward movement occurring before 1998.[2]

Determinants of the Medium-Term Path of the Real Exchange Rate

Modeling exchange rate dynamics is a daunting task because of the complexity of the forces determining exchange rates. Determining "equilibrium" exchange rates is even more of a challenge. These difficulties are further exacerbated in the case of developing economies where substantial structural changes can make the underlying relationships unstable. In the case of China, existing methodologies provide a wide range of estimates with a great deal of uncertainty attached to each of them. This subsection illustrates, on the basis of some commonly used techniques, how wide and imprecise the range of estimates of China's equilibrium exchange rate tends to be.

A number of recent studies have used a variety of methods to estimate the equilibrium exchange rate of

---

[2]Since China does not report export deflators or export unit values, three proxies are used: (1) deflator of manufacturing sector gross output; (2) deflator of manufacturing output in foreign-funded enterprises (FFEs), (since FFEs are concentrated in producing manufacturing exports); and (3) tradable goods prices in the CPI basket. Much of the underlying data used for calculating the proxies was only available since 1993.

the renminbi. Chou and Shih (1998) estimate the equilibrium exchange rate between 1978 and 1994 using both a purchasing power parity (PPP) approach and an approach based on the shadow price of foreign exchange, and find that the renminbi was overvalued for much of this period, but came close to equilibrium between 1990 and 1994. Zhang (2001) estimates a behavioral equilibrium exchange rate between 1952 and 1997 by using a set of fundamental determinants of the actual real exchange rate. He finds that the renminbi exchange rate was overvalued during most of the estimation period, but was close to its equilibrium in 1997. More recently, Funke and Rahn (2004) estimate a behavioral equilibrium exchange rate with quarterly data between 1985 and 2002 using a set of variables similar to the ones used in the present paper, and conclude that the renminbi was not substantially undervalued as of end-2002. Numerous market analysts have also estimated partial equilibrium models centered around trade equations and argue that the renminbi is currently undervalued, but the range of their estimates of the undervaluation is very wide.

We first use an extended relative PPP approach to explain movements in the real exchange rate, as measured by the CPI-based REER (Alberola and others (1999) use a similar approach). This approach incorporates the impact of relative productivity gains in the tradable and nontradable goods sectors (Balassa-Samuelson effects), as well as other fundamentals, on the real exchange rate (Bayoumi, Faruqee, and Lee, 2003).

The model specifies the real effective exchange rate as a function of:

- *Relative productivity gains,* proxied by changes in the CPI to PPI ratio in China relative to partner countries.[3] As described in Balassa (1964), faster productivity growth in the tradable goods sector relative to the nontradable goods sector compared to partner countries typically leads to an increase in nontradable goods prices relative to tradable goods prices in the home country and, hence, an appreciation of the real exchange rate.
- *Net foreign assets (NFAs).* A long-run decline in the NFA position (or a rise in the home country's indebtedness to the rest of the world) would require a larger trade surplus over the medium term to match the higher level of debt servicing, which, in turn, requires a more depreciated real exchange rate, and vice versa (Lane and Milesi-Ferretti, 2000).

---

[3]Direct measures of relative productivity are not available. Since PPI contains mainly tradable goods prices and CPI contains a substantial portion of nontradables, the CPI/PPI ratio is a function of relative prices of nontradable versus tradable goods.

Figure 4.4. Variables Used in the Estimation of the Medium-Term Exchange Rate

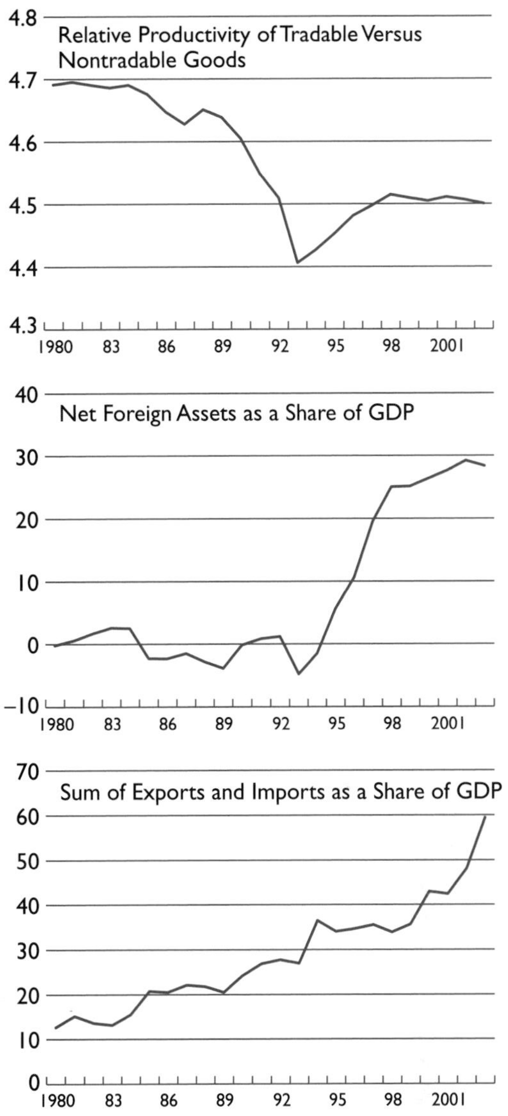

Source: IMF staff calculations.

- *Openness of the trade regime,* measured by the ratio of the sum of imports and exports to GDP. A more restrictive trade regime tends to be linked to a more appreciated currency.

Using a nonlinear least squares estimator approach, we estimate the above model using annual average data between 1980 and 2003. The variables in the model are plotted in Figure 4.4 and the key

Table 4.1. Medium-Term Determinants of the Real Exchange Rate: Extended Relative PPP Method

Variable	(1)	(2)	(3)
Constant	−0.42	−0.38	−1.82
	(0.28)	(0.28)	(0.86)
TNT	1.12	1.11	1.43
	(3.46)	(3.92)	(3.26)
NFA	0.90	0.91	1.01
	(3.03)	(3.2)	(2.33)
Open	−0.30	−0.30	−0.36
	(0.75)	(0.82)	(0.52)
dum	−37.28	−37.40	−38.19
	(2.55)	(2.7)	(2.81)
dum * TNT	8.30	8.33	8.44
	(2.67)	(2.8)	(2.92)
dum * NFA	−7.03	−7.03	−5.64
	(1.57)	(1.65)	(1.28)
dum * Open	−6.24	−6.23	−4.84
	(2.2)	(2.31)	(1.64)
Number of observations	24	24	24
Adjusted R-squared	0.96	0.97	0.97
S.E. of regression	0.06	0.06	0.05
F-statistic	51.20	61.91	54.63

Note: Absolute t-statistics are reported in parentheses below the coefficient estimates. Results in column (1) are from a nonlinear least squares specification, which adds lags of the first differences of the variables used in the ordinary least squares estimation and the lag of the equilibrium error to modify the OLS results. Column (2) represents results from a dynamic OLS specification, which adds leads and lags of the first differences of the explanatory variables to the OLS estimation. Column (3) is a modified version of column (2), omitting some leads that are not statistically significant.

Figure 4.5. Actual and Estimated CPI-Based REER
(1990 = 100)

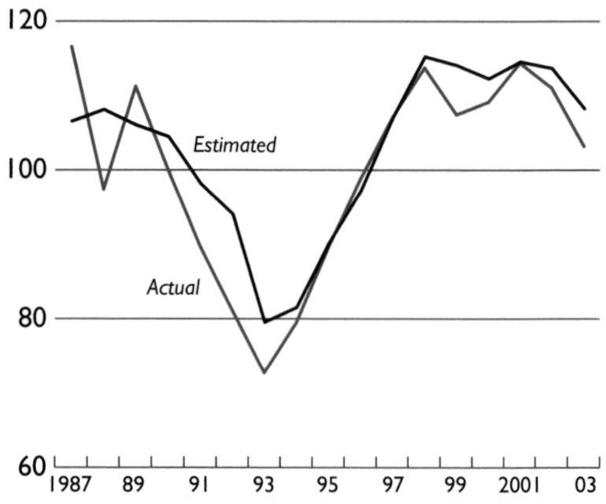

Source: IMF staff calculations.

results are summarized in Table 4.1, column (1). *REER* is the CPI-based real effective exchange rate; *TNT* is the relative productivity of tradable versus nontradable goods; *NFA* is the stock of net foreign assets (expressed as a ratio to GDP); *Open* is a measure of openness of the trade regime; and *d* is a dummy variable equal to 1 for 1980–86 and 0 otherwise.[4] *T*-statistics are in parentheses. The signs of the coefficients are in line with predictions of standard economic theories.[5] The estimated coefficients imply that a 1 percent increase in *TNT* would lead to a slightly more than 1 percent real appreciation, while a 1 percentage point increase in the *NFA* to GDP ratio is associated with a 0.9 percent higher real exchange rate. On the other hand, a 1 percentage point increase in the measure of trade openness would be associated with a 0.3 percent decline in the real value of the currency.

Alternative estimation methods generally confirmed the above results. Columns (2) and (3) in Table 4.1 display the results from two specifications of dynamic OLS estimators. In addition, various stability tests confirmed that the parameters of the estimated models are generally stable over the period 1987–2003. Nevertheless, the estimation results need to be interpreted with caution. The use of the relative CPI/PPI ratio as a proxy for relative productivity has some drawbacks. A better proxy might have been the ratio of the GDP deflator to the manufacturing deflator, but these data are not available. In addition, liberalization of price controls, which may have affected CPI and PPI at different times, could be misinterpreted in this methodology as changes in relative productivity.

A medium-term path of the real exchange rate is calculated using the coefficients from the nonlinear least square estimates and the realized values of the explanatory variables. This estimated path is plotted against the actual CPI-based REER in Figure 4.5.[6] While movements of the two series are generally in line, there are episodes during which there have been

---

[4]The *NFA* is calculated by adding accumulated current account surpluses to the estimated value of *NFA* in 1979. The dummy variable is used to capture the effects of major structural reforms and trade liberalization starting in 1987.

[5]Based on estimation results for the period 1987–2003.

---

[6]Results for the other equations estimated are qualitatively similar.

persistent differences between actual and estimated values. However, the differences in the past few years have not been large, which could be interpreted as an indication that the exchange rate may not be substantially undervalued. One should, of course, bear in mind that interpreting fitted values from estimation of such reduced-form equations as indicators of equilibrium exchange rates is fraught with conceptual problems.

An alternative approach to assessing real exchange rate levels that is commonly used is the macroeconomic balance approach (see Isard and Faruqee, 1998; and Isard and others, 2001). This approach examines the exchange rate from an equilibrium saving-investment balance point of view. It compares the "underlying" current account position (the position that would emerge at prevailing market exchange rates if all countries were producing at their potential output levels and the effects of past exchange rate changes have fed through) with an estimated "equilibrium" or "normal" position based on the medium-term determinants of saving and investment. The difference is then used to derive an estimate of how much the exchange rate would have to move (based on estimates of trade elasticities) to shift the underlying current account balance toward its medium-term norms.

Given the difficulties in estimating the underlying current account balance and an equilibrium saving-investment balance, especially for developing countries, some proxies have to be used for these concepts. In the case of China, the underlying current account is proxied by its recent average value, and two proxies are used for the equilibrium saving-investment balance. A norm for the equilibrium saving investment balance is derived from a panel data estimate of the determinants of the saving-investment balance using a set of structural and macroeconomic variables (norm A).[7] Another norm (norm B), is derived by estimating the current account balance that would stabilize the *NFA* to GDP ratio at the 2001 level.

As shown in Table 4.2, contrasting results come from comparing the underlying current account balance with two alternative norms. Norm A suggests that, given the current high saving rate, China should run larger current account surpluses than in the past, indicating a need for a real exchange rate depreciation. On the other hand, norm B would require China to run lower current account surpluses (1 percent of

---

[7]Norm A is derived using coefficients obtained from an econometric study of medium-term determinants of current accounts using a panel dataset for an extensive group of developing countries (Chinn and Prasad, 2003). The variables in the estimated equation include stage of development, *NFA* position, dependency ratio, and financial deepening.

Table 4.2. Measures of Underlying Current Account Balances and Norms
(In percent of GDP)

Underlying Current Account Balance	Current Account Balance "Norms"	
Average for 2000–2002	Norm A	Norm B
2.10	3.10	0.98

Sources: State Administration of Foreign Exchange; and IMF staff estimates.

GDP) than in the past, suggesting the need for a real exchange rate appreciation.

The basic conclusion to be drawn from these alternative methodologies is that it is difficult to arrive at any firm and robust conclusion about the equilibrium level of the renminbi using existing techniques. Furthermore, as discussed below, the medium-term path of the exchange rate is crucially dependent on the sources of shocks hitting the economy.

Sources of Real Exchange Rate Fluctuations

A different approach to understanding the dynamics of the real exchange rate is to study its long-run and short-run movements in a unified framework, where it is modeled as an endogenous variable that responds to various structural shocks. This could provide a better understanding of the evolution of real exchange rates. To this end, a structural vector autoregression (VAR) model following Clarida and Gali (1994) is used to estimate the relative importance of different macroeconomic shocks to real exchange rate movements in China. This approach has the benefit of allowing all variables to be simultaneously determined by structural shocks in the short run while, in order to successfully estimate the model, a few of the long-run relationships are pinned down on the basis of specific theoretical models.

Questions may arise as to whether this type of empirical model is applicable to a developing economy such as China. For example, the model assumes an open economy with a flexible exchange rate and capital mobility, and full employment in the long run. While China may not fully satisfy these assumptions, fundamental changes in the economy over the past two decades have made the model increasingly more relevant. Starting from a closed, centrally planned economy in the early 1980s, China has

Box 4.1. Identification of Shocks in a Structural VAR Model

Vector autoregressions (VARs) have become a popular empirical tool for modeling various macroeconomic relationships. However, achieving statistical identification in these models requires strong restrictions on the short-run relationships among the variables in the system. This poses a problem when modeling relationships where it is difficult to plausibly argue that one variable is "exogenous" relative to another in the short run. For instance, output and prices jointly respond to different shocks and viewing either of these as "predetermined" relative to the other makes little sense in most contexts. Furthermore, when including the exchange rate in such a system, the notion of shocks such as an "exchange rate shock" has little meaning since, in principle, it is the exchange rate that responds to different underlying shocks.

The structural VAR approach, originally developed by Blanchard and Quah (1989) to study the joint dynamics of output and prices, provides a way around these problems. This technique allows a VAR to be identified using a minimal set of long-run restrictions that are derived from economic theory. The variables in the model are then allowed to respond to underlying ("structural") shocks in a completely unrestricted manner in the short run.

Clarida and Gali (1994) extended the Blanchard-Quah approach to one that allows for an analysis of real exchange rate dynamics in an open economy setting based on the Mundell-Fleming-Dornbusch analytical framework. The basic VAR includes three variables—log differences of (1) relative output, (2) relative CPI, and (3) the real exchange rate. Since both domestic and foreign macroeconomic conditions affect the real exchange rate, the output growth and inflation variables for the home country are measured relative to the corresponding partner country variables (in a manner consistent with the construction of the real exchange rate

variable). Three structural shocks are then identified by the model—relative supply shocks, relative real demand shocks, and relative nominal demand shocks. Each of these shocks affects all of the variables in the short and long run.

The short-run relationships among the three variables are unconstrained. In order to identify the model, however, three of the nine long-run relationships between the shocks and the variables need to be restricted. These restrictions, derived from a stochastic open economy macroeconomic model, are that:
- The relative nominal demand shock has no long-run effect on the *level* of the real exchange rate.
- The relative nominal and real demand shocks have no long-run effects on the *level* of relative output.

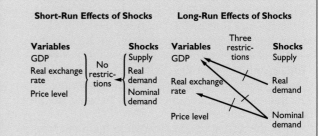

Short-Run Effects of Shocks   **Long-Run Effects of Shocks**

Thus, in this setup, there are no restrictions on the short-run responses of the real exchange rate to the three structural shocks. Of the three possible long-run responses of the real exchange rate, only one is restricted to be zero, and this is an entirely plausibl restriction since it is hard to imagine that nominal shocks (e.g., money supply shocks) could permanently alter the *level* of the real exchange rate.

opened up its trade and become more market oriented. Price controls have been all but eliminated. Even when the renminbi was officially fixed, the nominal exchange rate moved frequently to reflect the economic developments and the rate prevailing in the black market or swap market. Capital controls were never watertight, and flows in the form of foreign direct investment and external borrowing were significant through much of the estimation period. In recent years, capital movements have become increasingly large, as reflected in the large outflow during the Asian crisis and the sharp reversal in the last two-three years. While China is still far from full employment, output capacity cannot be easily expanded in the short run. Given these considerations, it is not unreasonable to use this model to disentangle various sources of shocks and to examine

whether the model's predictions apply in the case of China.[8]

A three-variable structural VAR is estimated using annual data for the period 1980–2002. The variables in the VAR are relative output, the real effective exchange rate, and the relative price level.[9] The variables are expressed relative to those in trading part-

---

[8]A number of recent studies have applied similar structural VAR models to developing economies, including Chen and Wu (1997) on Korea, Taiwan Province of China, and the Philippines; Borda, Manioc, and Montauban (2000) on the Caribbean countries; Hoffmaister and Roldós (2001) on Brazil and Korea; and Dibooglu and Kutan (2001) on Poland and Hungary.

[9]For a description of the SVAR methodology, model specification, data calculations, and more detailed estimation results, see Wang (2004).

Figure 4.6. Accumulated Impulse Response Functions for the Real Effective Exchange Rate
(In percent)

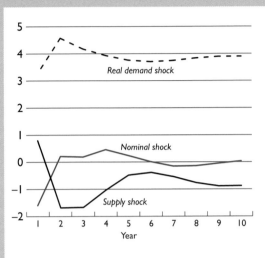

Source: IMF staff calculations.
Note: Since the model is estimated in first differences, the resulting impulse responses were cumulated in order to derive the effects of the structural shocks on the level of the REER. The long-run level response of the REER to a nominal shock is restricted to be zero. There are no other restrictions on the short-run and long-run responses of the REER to different shocks.

Figure 4.7. Decomposition of Forecast Errors of Real Exchange Rate
(In percent)

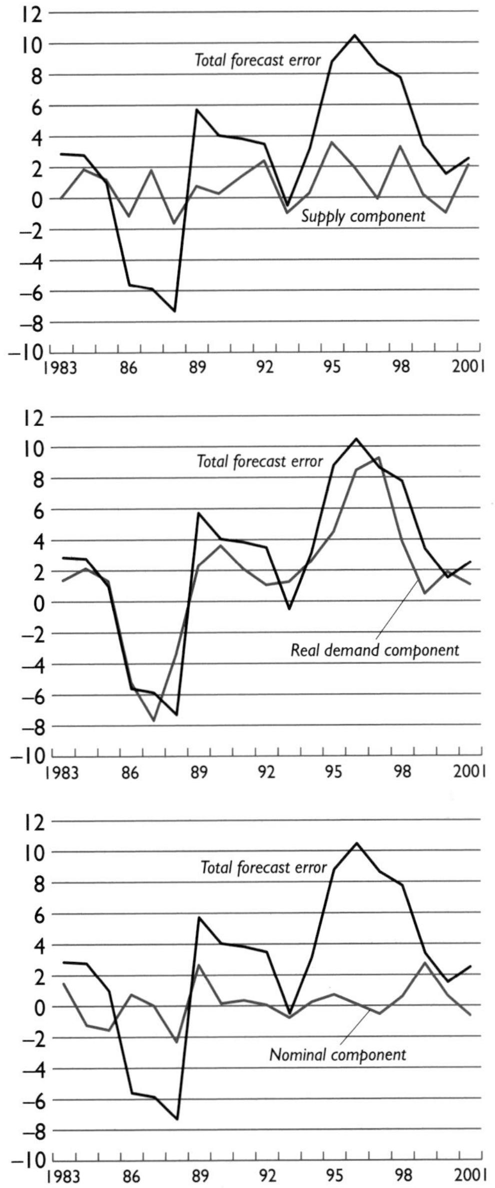

Source: IMF staff estimates.
Note: Total forecast error is the difference between the actual real exchange rate and forecasts based on history up to 1983 and cumulated effects of the various shocks thereafter. Supply, demand, and nominal components sum to total forecast error.

ner countries because both domestic and external macroeconomic conditions affect the real exchange rate. Three types of shocks are identified, and in the traditional IS-LM framework, these could be referred to as aggregate supply shocks, aggregate demand shocks, and nominal demand shocks (shocks affecting the money market). More details on the methodology are provided in Box 4.1 (also see Wang, 2004).

Figure 4.6 displays the impulse response functions of the level of the real effective exchange rate to one standard deviation structural shocks. As predicted by standard economic theory, a positive supply shock leads to a short-term appreciation followed by a decline in the real exchange rate in the long run, while a positive real demand shock is associated with a permanent appreciation of the real exchange rate. A nominal shock has a temporary (depreciating) impact on the real exchange rate with no long-run effects—as imposed by the long-run restriction.

The structural decomposition indicates that real shocks accounted for most of the variation in real exchange rate changes during the estimation period, whereas nominal shocks were less important. Real

demand shocks are the most important factor, especially in the short run, and account for about half of the variance in exchange rate changes even in the long run; supply shocks also have a significant contribution that rises over longer horizons. Of course, these results should be interpreted with caution, given significant changes that are likely to have occurred in the structure of the economy.

Nevertheless, the overall importance of real shocks to the variations of real exchange rate changes is consistent with findings for other developing countries (for example, Ahmed, 2003). Compared with studies on industrial countries with flexible exchange rate systems (Clarida and Gali, 1994; and Chadha and Prasad, 1997), supply shocks here play a more important role, maybe because China has been going through rather major supply-side changes such as structural reforms and productivity shocks. Moreover, nominal shocks appear not to have played as large a role as in other countries in explaining the fluctuations in either output growth or real exchange rate movements, possibly because China has a de facto fixed exchange rate system with a relatively closed capital account. Hoffmaister and Roldós (2001) also find that supply shocks contribute more than nominal shocks to the fluctuations of changes in the real exchange rate in the case of Korea.

Using the estimated VAR, a historical decomposition was derived to examine whether or not the supply, demand, and nominal shocks that had bee identified could plausibly explain the time path followed by the renminbi real exchange rate over the last two decades. Figure 4.7 displays the "historical" decomposition of forecast errors of the real exchange rate. The solid line in each panel is the total forecast error—the difference between the actual real exchange rate and forecasts based on history up to 1983 and cumulated effects of the various shocks thereafter. The dotted lines are contributions of individual shocks to the total forecast error.

It seems that we can indeed verify that episodes of tight money or positive real demand shocks were associated with real appreciations of the renminbi. For example, real demand factors rose sharply between 1993 and 1997, coinciding with the sharp appreciation of the renminbi. As the onset of the Asian crisis sharply reduced external demand for China's products, relative demand factors declined starting in 1998. However, nominal factors (relatively tight monetary conditions) and supply factors (major restructuring of state-owned enterprises that started in 1997 and could have had a temporary disruptive impact on production) kept the real exchange rate from depreciating more than it did. More recently, supply-side factors pushed up the real exchange rate in 2001; these are probably linked with strong inflows of foreign direct investment on account of productivity gains in China.

This analysis indicates that it is possible to reasonably model fluctuations in China's real exchange rate using a conventional framework. But it also shows the importance of properly accounting for the sources of shocks in trying to understand short-run and medium-run exchange rate dynamics.

V   Medium-Term Fiscal Challenges

Annalisa Fedelino and Raju Jan Singh

China's current fiscal position appears relatively sound. Both its overall budget deficit (3 percent of GDP in 2003) and debt as a ratio to GDP (about 26 percent in 2003) compare well with those of a group of emerging market countries, although differences in coverage and data quality need to be taken into account when comparing data across countries (Table 5.1).[1] While China's primary fiscal position may appear weaker than in comparator countries, strong economic growth and low domestic interest rates have so far partially counteracted the possible adverse impact of sustained primary deficits on debt dynamics.

Despite its current position of relative strength, however, China faces important fiscal challenges in the course of its transition to a market economy. Over the medium term, the government is likely to have to shoulder various costs related to the restructuring of a still largely state-owned economy; the cost of recapitalizing state-owned banks; the funding of social security for a rapidly aging population; possible liabilities, explicit as well as contingent, that subnational governments are contracting, especially related to large-scale infrastructure projects; and significant government programs to address increasing regional disparities, including the need for increased spending for health and education (Nehru and others, 1997; and Lardy, 2000). China's strong macroeconomic conditions provide a propitious environment in which to tackle these liabilities. If not addressed, these liabilities will continue to increase and may call for significant government interventions under less favorable macroeconomic

Table 5.1. Selected Countries: Comparison of Public Debt and Fiscal Positions, Average 2000–02
(In percent of GDP)

	Public Debt	Overall Balance	Primary Balance
China	24.4	−3.4	−2.6
EMBI countries[1]	64.5	−4.0	1.2
Of which: emerging Asia[2]	71.4	−3.4	1.6

Source: IMF, *World Economic Outlook.*
[1]Includes 27 emerging market countries covered by the JP Morgan Emerging Market Bond Index.
[2]Including India, Indonesia, Korea, Malaysia, Philippines, and Thailand.

conditions sometime in the future, thereby potentially creating serious economic dislocations.

Against this background, this section briefly illustrates the main fiscal developments in the last few years, highlights progress in fiscal reforms, and lays out the important challenges for the future. The main conclusion is that, while China's current fiscal position appears healthy, its fiscal sustainability outlook could be altered by the possible impact of substantial contingent claims on the central government and deviations from the currently very favorable macroeconomic conditions.

Recent Fiscal Developments

China's fiscal position in the last five years has been marked by a sharp change from previous trends. Steadily declining trends in both revenue and expenditure from the early 1980s to the mid-1990s have been reversed, but with a faster expansion in expenditure than in revenue, thus resulting in larger

---

[1]China's external debt, at about 5 percent of GDP, compares favorably to the average for emerging market countries of about 36 percent of GDP. The average in emerging Asia is lower, at 24 percent of GDP—but still considerably higher than in China. However, coverage of debt statistics varies across countries. In China, government debt is mostly domestic and denominated in local currency. It includes liabilities of the central government; local governments are not allowed to borrow by law, although they can be recipients of onlending from the center.

Figure 5.1. Revenue, Expenditure, and Fiscal Balance
(In percent of GDP)

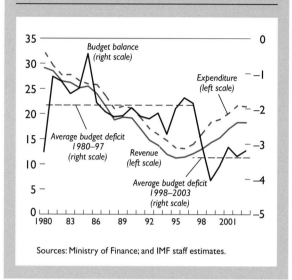

Sources: Ministry of Finance; and IMF staff estimates.

budget deficits on average.[2] Reflecting the fiscal stimulus policies adopted in the wake of the Asian crisis, the budget deficit "jumped" to a new level in 1998; and it has since remained around 3 percent of GDP (Figure 5.1).[3]

The revenue gains, from a low of 11.2 percent of GDP in 1995 to an estimated 18.8 percent of GDP in 2003, have largely reflected strong growth in tax collections, in particular in value-added tax (VAT) and income taxes (Table 5.2). In addition to buoyant economic activity, the revenue boost may be attributed to two main factors: a reform package introduced in 1994 and improvements in tax administration. The 1994 reform modified the revenue-sharing system between the center and subnational governments in favor of the center (for a background discussion, see Section VI); simplified the tax system, by replacing the multitier system of turnover taxes with a VAT; and reformed tax administration, by splitting the tax bureau into two levels—the State Administration of Taxation, responsible for collecting central and shared taxes, and a local tax administration in charge of collecting local revenue. This last measure, by removing central and shared taxes from local administration, has largely eliminated opportunities to divert central revenue via manipulation of tax assessments.

[2]The expansion, however, has also been affected by the inclusion in the budget of previously off-budgeted revenue and expenditure.

[3]Fiscal data in China remain subject to limitations. Budgetary data exclude spending associated with onlending to local governments, both domestic and external. Data on social and extrabudgetary funds are provided annually and with a long lag. Expenditure is classified by function, and no economic classification is available.

Table 5.2. State Budget Revenue[1]

	1997	1998	1999	2000	2001	2002	2003 Estimate
	(In percent of GDP)						
Total revenue	12.1	13.0	14.3	15.3	17.0	18.3	18.8
Tax revenue	11.1	11.8	13.0	14.1	15.7	16.8	17.1
Of which:							
Taxes on income and profits	2.1	2.0	2.3	2.9	4.0	4.5	...
Value-added tax on domestic goods	4.4	4.6	4.7	5.1	5.5	5.9	6.2
VAT and excises on imports	0.7	0.7	1.2	1.7	1.7	1.8	2.4
Nontax revenue	1.1	1.2	1.3	1.2	1.3	1.5	1.6
	(As a share of total revenue)						
Tax revenue	91.3	90.7	91.0	92.0	92.3	91.9	91.3
Of which:							
Taxes on income and profits	17.2	15.4	16.4	19.2	23.6	24.6	...
Value-added tax on domestic goods	36.4	35.5	33.1	33.3	32.3	32.2	33.0
VAT and excises on imports	5.6	5.4	8.7	10.9	10.0	9.8	12.7
Nontax revenue	8.7	9.3	9.0	8.0	7.7	8.1	8.7

Sources: Ministry of Finance; State Administration of Taxation; and IMF staff estimates.
[1]The coverage of these data includes the central government, provinces, municipalities, and counties.

Table 5.3. State Budget Expenditure[1]

	1997	1998	1999	2000	2001	2002	2003 Estimate
			(In percent of GDP)				
Total expenditure and net lending	14.0	16.1	18.3	18.9	20.1	21.7	21.6
Current expenditure	11.5	12.6	13.7	14.7	16.1	17.3	17.4
Of which:							
Administration and defense	2.7	3.8	4.1	4.4	4.9	5.5	...
Culture, education, public health,							
and science	2.7	2.7	3.1	3.2	3.6	4.0	3.8
Pensions and social welfare relief	0.2	0.2	1.0	1.7	2.0	2.5	...
Capital expenditure	2.2	2.6	3.5	3.3	3.6	3.9	3.9
Unrecorded expenditure	0.3	0.9	1.2	0.8	0.4	0.4	0.4
Memorandum item:							
Primary expenditure	13.2	15.1	17.6	18.1	19.3	21.0	20.8
			(As a share of total revenue)				
Current expenditure	82.5	78.3	74.7	77.8	79.9	80.0	80.5
Of which:							
Administration and defense	19.4	23.5	22.6	23.4	24.6	25.4	...
Culture, education, public health,							
and science	19.0	16.9	16.7	16.9	17.9	18.3	17.8
Pensions and social welfare relief	1.4	1.4	5.5	9.1	9.9	11.6	...
Capital expenditure	15.6	15.9	18.8	17.7	17.9	18.1	17.5
Unrecorded expenditure	1.9	5.8	6.5	4.4	2.2	1.8	1.6
Memorandum item:							
Primary expenditure	94.3	94.2	96.0	95.7	95.9	97.0	96.2

Sources: Ministry of Finance; and IMF staff estimates.
[1]The coverage of these data includes the central government, provinces, municipalities, and counties.

Improved tax administration has played a crucial role in strengthening revenue performance in China, especially in view of the challenges posed by the transformation from a centrally planned economy to a socialist market economy with a decentralized fiscal structure. Under the central planning system, taxpayers, most notably state-owned enterprises (SOEs) and collective farms, were relatively small in number and could be easily monitored. In a market economy with a decentralized administrative structure, not only are there many more taxpayers, but they also cannot be as easily monitored from the center. For example, it is estimated that, in the rural sector, the government shifted from collecting taxes from about 50,000 communes to more than 200 million households and over one million town and village enterprises (Wong, 1997). Among other reforms, the "golden tax" project (computerization of the VAT collection) has significantly contributed to increased revenue. Finally, steps have been taken to bring off-budget revenue on budget through the extension of budget coverage to previously excluded government units and through the tax-for-fees reform.[4]

The revenue increase has allowed a gradual expansion in expenditure programs, from a recent minimum of about 13 percent of GDP in 1996 to an estimated 21.6 percent of GDP in 2003 (Table 5.3).[5] The largest increases have been recorded in areas targeted by the government's development policies. For example, expenditure on pension and social welfare programs increased by about 2 percent of GDP over this period, as some social expenditure mandates previously assigned to SOEs were trans-

---

[4]The tax-for-fees reform was initiated in 2000 as a measure to boost incomes in rural areas. It aims at the elimination of the many unofficial fees levied by local governments while remaining fees are being converted into taxes and subject to caps mandated by the center.

[5]"Estimated" refers to official estimate, modified for some adjustments applied by the IMF staff, including onlending to local governments, external borrowing excluded from the budget, and subsidies to SOEs.

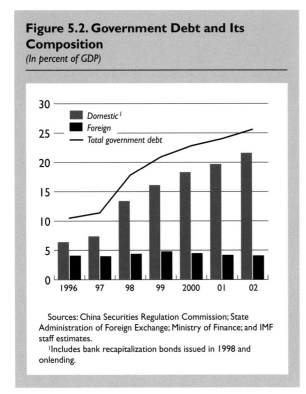

Figure 5.2. Government Debt and Its Composition
(In percent of GDP)

Sources: China Securities Regulation Commission; State Administration of Foreign Exchange; Ministry of Finance; and IMF staff estimates.
[1]Includes bank recapitalization bonds issued in 1998 and onlending.

improving the budget classification system and extending the budget coverage to extrabudgetary activities. These ongoing reforms should contribute to improved expenditure management and more efficient expenditure policies.

Since the use of central bank overdrafts was discontinued in 1994 and recourse to foreign financing has remained limited, the rising budget deficits have been covered mainly by issuance of government paper. Hence, the stock of government debt has gradually increased over the last few years, reaching about 26 percent of GDP at end-2002 (Figure 5.2). As foreign debt has remained stable at less than 5 percent of GDP over the period, the issuance of government paper accounts for most of the growth in government debt. The sharp increase in debt in 1998 is also due to the issuance of bank recapitalization bonds, equivalent to 3.4 percent of GDP.

Medium-Term Challenges

Despite the broadly favorable fiscal position currently enjoyed by China, the government stock of debt would be significantly larger if a number of liabilities—direct as well as contingent—were to be assumed by the central government.[8] These include nonperforming loans (NPLs)—in case of financial distress, state banks may need to be bailed out by the government;[9] unfunded pension obligations; and liability-creating activities of SOEs and local governments (Daniel and others, 2003). All these obligations may need to be settled by the government in the future in the absence of sustained reforms or changes in the current fiscal management system.

A preliminary assessment based on officially reported NPLs at end-2003 suggests that potential losses from NPLs could amount to about 13 percent of GDP for the four big state commercial banks alone (see Section VII for more details on NPLs). This figure is based on a reported NPL stock of 16 percent of GDP and an assumed recovery rate equivalent to that achieved so far by asset management companies (21½ percent). However, potential weaknesses in reporting and inevitable problems in implementing new prudential regimes, especially in some of the smaller banks, suggest that the existing stock

ferred back to the government. Similarly, capital expenditure has expanded by about 1.5 percent of GDP over the last five years. There was also an increase in expenditure for administration and defense, by almost 3 percent of GDP, matched by a similar increase in outlays for culture, education, public health, and science.[6]

Although not as far-reaching as the 1994 reform package on the revenue side, various reforms have been incrementally introduced on the expenditure side as well. Starting in 1999, a blueprint for reforms in public expenditure management was adopted, resulting in the restructuring of the Ministry of Finance, the creation of a treasury department, and the establishment of a single treasury account at the central level and its extension to the subnational level.[7] Work is also under way on

---

[6]The current budget classification, which is being upgraded, does not provide an accurate description of expenditure by economic and functional types. Hence, it is difficult to explain past trends in expenditure programs.

[7]A standard treasury single account (TSA) is a bank account or a set of linked bank accounts through which the government, including its entities and spending units, transacts all receipts and payments, and consolidates its cash balances. Cash balances held by a government are efficiently centralized through a TSA.

---

[8]A contingent liability is an obligation triggered by a discrete but uncertain event. For example, a loan guaranteed by the central government becomes the latter's explicit obligation when the guarantee is called.

[9]There may also be pressure on the government to protect depositors, regardless of the ownership of banks, in the absence of a deposit insurance scheme.

of NPLs could be significantly higher. In addition, while efforts are being made to reduce the flow of new NPLs through SOE and financial sector reforms, part of ongoing bank lending could become nonperforming over the next few years (see also Karacadag, 2003).

Estimates of the government's pension liabilities vary a great deal, depending on assumptions regarding reforms to be introduced into the system. The current pension system, reflecting previous reforms, has three pillars comprising a public pension, mandatory individual pension accounts, and supplementary voluntary individual accounts. The system has an increasing cash deficit due to a relatively high replacement rate (ratio of retirement benefit to earned income) and the need to finance pension liabilities of the old system. As a result, the individual accounts are largely notional, with current contributions being used to meet current payment obligations. If this pay-as-you-go practice is maintained, the deficit will widen as the ratio of contributors to beneficiaries declines further as the population ages.

The World Bank estimates that the transition cost of shifting from the present system to fully funded individual accounts could amount to a net present value of 70 percent of GDP (over the next 75 years) if the parameters in the retirement system remain unchanged (Dorfman and Sin, 2001). Even relatively marginal reforms could drastically alter these costs if undertaken in the next few years. For example, the financing gap could be lowered to about 7 percent of GDP through a number of parametric changes, including raising the retirement age to 65 and indexing pensions to inflation rather than wages. The remaining financing gap could be covered from sources other than payroll contributions, for example privatization proceeds.

The restructuring of SOEs could also translate into significant government liabilities. First, while part of the borrowings by SOEs and semigovernmental finance companies does not carry any explicit government guarantee, it could nevertheless become a liability for the central government in the future in case these entities are unable to discharge their financial obligations.[10] Second, social obligations of SOEs (such as the provision of education and health services and pensions) have been progressively transferred to local governments (see Section VI). Again, payments for these obligations may become

the responsibility of the center in case local governments experience financial difficulties.

While subnational governments are banned by law from borrowing directly, they have effective recourse to bank borrowing and bond issuance through public enterprises, especially to fund large infrastructure projects. This indirect financing carries fiscal risks for both local governments and, ultimately, the central government. For example, public infrastructure is largely financed by bank loans. Where these projects have limited repayment capacity, or where profits are subject to other commitments (e.g., cross subsidization of loss-making highways), difficulties in servicing debts may translate into direct government intervention to bail out these projects. Estimates of the size of these contingent liabilities are, however, not available.

There are also substantial requirements for additional public spending in the coming years to meet social needs. Although infrastructure spending has significantly expanded over the past years, the OECD (2002b) reports that spending on education and other social programs is still falling short of comparable international levels.[11] Moreover, expenditure needs over the next decade for health (especially as the population ages), education, and environment protection will increase further. China's recent accession to the World Trade Organization will also require additional government resources to facilitate the adjustments implied by trade and investment liberalization, such as retraining displaced workers. Although the uncertainties are large, the OECD estimated that government primary expenditure would need to increase by at least an additional 2 percent to 3 percent of GDP over the next five to ten years to accommodate these needs.

Despite these rising spending pressures and the costs of addressing some contingent liabilities, it would appear that only limited fiscal adjustment would be needed to avoid pushing the government debt-to-GDP ratio on to an unsustainable path. However, this conclusion is based on the important assumptions of continued rapid economic growth and no incurrence of new quasi-fiscal liabilities by the government.

At the same time, the government has substantial assets, which it could sell to meet some of its quasi-

---

[10]For example, the Guangdong Trust and Investment Corporation was declared bankrupt and closed without a bailout of most of its creditors in 1999. Nonetheless, the provincial government decided to repay individual depositors, although covering only a very small amount of their claims.

[11]For example, China spends about 3 percent of GDP on education. This is slightly below the average for Asian countries (excluding Japan) at 3.4 percent of GDP, but compares less favorably with higher levels observed among some other countries in the region—for example, in India (above 4 percent of GDP), Thailand (above 5 percent of GDP), and Malaysia (above 6 percent of GDP). In OECD countries, the average is 6 percent of GDP (OECD, 2002b).

Box 5.1. An Assessment of China's State Equity Share in SOEs

In China, the state has an ownership share in over 150,000 state-owned enterprises (SOEs), of which more than 1,000 are listed on stock exchanges in China and overseas. The value of these assets has important implications for fiscal sustainability, as proceeds from some asset sales are already designated to partially fund government pensions and future sales could contribute also to covering additional government obligations.

It is difficult, however, to estimate the value of these assets, due to lack of comprehensive and independently verified financial information on SOEs. Nevertheless, illustrative estimates can be derived using balance sheet and income data for the SOEs and various stock market indicators. These estimates are sensitive to key assumptions and yield a wide range of results on the net value of state equity share in the SOEs, from zero to 100 percent of GDP. Other studies suggest valuations ranging from 25 percent to 65 percent of GDP (see, e.g., Studwell, 2000; and Bottelier, 2002). While the wide range of these estimates highlights the uncertainties, it suggests that the state probably has sizable assets.

Assessing the State's Stake in SOEs

Various methods can be used to estimate the value of the state's equity stake in SOEs. Book value data suggest that SOEs are worth about 50–75 percent of GDP. The upper bound estimate is based on Ministry of Finance data, showing a book value of the state's equity stake in nonfinancial enterprises of about 65 percent of GDP in recent years, with an additional 10 percent of GDP equity in financial and overseas enterprises. However, nonfinancial enterprises reported that "unhealthy assets" (including actual and potential asset write-downs, such as delayed receivables, delayed depreciation, and excess inventories) were equivalent to almost one-third of equity. Therefore, adjusting for "unhealthy assets" gives a lower bound estimate of about 50 percent of GDP.

Book value estimates may, however, understate the market value of the SOE assets. In other emerging market economies, the market value of companies listed on the stock exchanges has generally been larger than their book value. For 19 emerging market economies, excluding China, the ratio of the market to book value was 1.6 in 2001 (see Tenev, Zhang, and Brefort, 2002). Applying this average ratio to the adjusted book value of China's SOE assets gives an estimated market value of about 80 percent of GDP.

In contrast, some studies suggest that China's SOEs may overvalue their assets and understate their liabilities, implying a much lower book value for the SOEs. Lardy (1998) and Steinfeld (2000) have argued that SOEs overvalue fixed assets and inventories by using very low depreciation rates and not adjusting the value of excessive inventories to fully reflect market prices. Moreover, exclusion of pension obligations and other contingencies would understate liabilities. For example, a downward adjustment in the book value of gross assets by one-third would wipe out the equity stake.

An alternative approach is to apply different price/earnings (P/E) ratios of Chinese listed companies to profits of SOEs. Assuming a P/E ratio of 20 (about the level used for initial public offerings of SOE shares issued on domestic stock markets in recent years) for listed and unlisted SOEs gives an estimated equity stake of about 50 percent of GDP, based on 2002 data. Assuming a P/E ratio of 15, in line with that prevailing for mainland companies that are listed on the Hong Kong SAR stock exchange, gives an estimate of 35 percent of GDP, while using the P/E ratio prevailing on Shanghai and Shenzhen stock markets of 40 gives an estimate of 100 percent of GDP. The latter estimate, however, probably overstates the state's equity share since (1) the P/E ratio on the mainland is artificially high because capital controls restrict offshore investment by domestic investors; (2) less than one-third of shares in individual listed companies are tradable, since the state holds the remaining equity; and (3) evidence from a Ministry of Finance survey suggests that more than half of the SOEs covered had overstated their profits by 10 percent or more (Ministry of Finance, 2002).

Using the price/sales ratios prevailing in other stock markets provides another method to estimate the state's equity share in the SOEs. For example, the price/sales ratio for H-shares and Red Chips in Hong Kong SAR of about 1.25 gives a valuation for SOEs of about 100 percent of GDP. This estimate would be lowered to about 70 percent of GDP if the price/sales ratio from emerging market economies is used. But these estimates may also overstate the value of unlisted SOEs, as these tend to be relatively unprofitable companies. The profits (before interest) of listed companies were around 10 percent of sales in 2002, almost three times those of unlisted companies.

Implications of State Assets for Fiscal Policy

The divestiture of state assets may provide significant funding for liabilities, but their valuation is uncertain and subject to a multitude of claims. In particular, while the book value of equity in SOEs is about evenly split between the central and local governments, the central government carries the responsibility for most of the explicit and contingent liabilities. Local governments have an incentive to dispose of assets and use the funds for their own purposes, rather than for funding central government liabilities. In addition, other parties could lay claim to funds generated from sales of shares in SOEs, including companies themselves wanting investment capital, and redundant and retired workers wanting payouts. Furthermore, the ability of Chinese financial markets to absorb large amounts from asset sales in a short period may be limited. All these factors suggest that the amount available to fund central government liabilities may be considerably less than the total net worth of state assets.

The establishment of the State Assets Supervision and Administration Commission in March 2003 should improve the management and oversight of nonfinancial SOEs. In particular, increased public disclosure of their accounts and the state's equity claim would also serve to improve public accountability for the management of these assets.

Prepared by Ray Brooks.

fiscal liabilities (Box 5.1). In fact, part of the remaining state shares in some of the publicly listed companies have already been earmarked to fund pension liabilities. Privatization of other SOEs would also allow the government to raise funds to offset its liabilities. However, the value of the state assets is highly uncertain; valuations for China's state equity share in the SOE sector vary greatly, from 25 percent to 100 percent of GDP. While this suggests that the government does have valuable assets, their divestiture may not raise significant amounts in domestic markets that are not deep and have a limited capacity to absorb a substantial volume of sales. The eventual realization value for these assets will depend crucially on strengthening management and implementing reforms in SOEs ahead of actual divestitures.

Conclusions

China's strong growth performance, the strength and potential of its domestic market, the availability of considerable domestic savings, and the large endowment of government assets are some of the elements that make its fiscal position, current and prospective, relatively strong. However, these elements do not provide sufficient reasons to avoid addressing past and incipient liabilities that may ultimately fall on the central government. China's current position of relative strength provides a unique opportunity to start addressing some of these liabilities and create room for their payment, if and when needed. The authorities' intention to adhere to a path of gradual fiscal consolidation over the medium term is a step in the right direction.

VI Fiscal Federalism

Annalisa Fedelino and Raju Jan Singh

The increased decentralization of intergovernmental fiscal relations since the early 1980s has played an important role in supporting the process of transition to a market economy and promoting growth in China. Some scholars have suggested that the devolution of authority from the center to local governments has contributed to China's spectacular growth performance over the last two decades (Box 6.1).

At the same time, however, China's impressive growth performance has not benefited all provinces equally.[1] Large income disparities remain across provinces; for example, in 2002 the highest provincial per capita income level was more than ten times greater than the lowest (Table 6.1). Among the top ten richest provinces, nine were in the east, while the ten poorest were in the central and western regions. Furthermore, the provision of public services is skewed in favor of richer provinces: for example, annual per capita healthcare expenditure varies from a maximum of about RMB 200 in Beijing and Shanghai to less than RMB 20 in the central provinces of Henan and Hunan. The role of center-local relations in perpetuating these disparities has come under increasing scrutiny.

Local governments are largely responsible for public service delivery and implementation of social policies. However, a widening gap is emerging between local governments' expenditure mandates (accounting for about 70 percent of total budgetary expenditure), which are assigned by the center, and resources immediately available to local governments (about 45 percent of total budgetary revenue, before transfers from the center). This imbalance implies that local governments, which are not allowed to borrow directly and whose transfers from the center are inadequate, experience difficulties in

Table 6.1. Per Capita Income Levels of Selected Provinces, 2002

	In Renminbi	In U.S. Dollars[1]	As a Ratio to Maximum
Top two provinces			
Shanghai	33,285	4,010	100.0
Beijing	22,577	2,720	67.8
Bottom two provinces			
Guizhou	3,088	372	9.3
Guangxi	5,092	613	15.3
Memorandum item:			
National average	9,255	1,115	27.8

Sources: *China Finance Yearbook, 2003;* and IMF staff calculations.
[1]At the exchange rate of US$1 = RMB 8.3.

financing basic services, and more so in poorer provinces where revenue is lower (Ahmad and others, 2004). This largely reflects the design as well as the implementation of the system of intergovernmental fiscal relations introduced in 1994. This system has not kept pace with the challenges posed by the process of transition to a market economy and growing regional disparities.

Against this background, this section looks at the main elements of the 1994 reform, focusing on revenue assignments, expenditure mandates, and the transfer system, mainly at the provincial level. The main conclusion is that, ten years into the reform, there is a pressing need to reexamine some aspects of intergovernmental fiscal relations, in particular the design and clarity of expenditure mandates and the transparency and efficiency of the transfer system.

The 1994 Fiscal Reform

Recentralization of Revenue

The core element of the 1994 reform was to ensure higher revenue as a ratio to GDP while also boosting

---

[1]China's government structure has four subnational (local) levels: the first tier consists of provincial level authorities (22 provinces, five autonomous regions, and four municipalities—Beijing, Shanghai, Tienjin, and Chongqing). The second tier comprises prefecture level authorities (some 330 prefectures and cities at prefecture level). The third tier encompasses more than 2,100 counties/cities at the county level, while the fourth tier includes about 48,000 villages/townships—overall, some 50,000 entities.

Box 6.1. Intergovernmental Fiscal Relations and Market Reforms in China: A Review of the Literature

The *market-preserving fiscal federalism* school is based on the idea that fiscal decentralization has provided local governments with significant incentives to promote growth (see, among others, Qian and Weingast, 1997; and Blanchard and Shleifer, 2001). More recently, Jin, Qian, and Weingast (2003a and 2003b) have tested the relationship between provincial governments' fiscal incentives and regional development over the period 1970–92. There are two results relevant to the analysis in this section. First, fiscal incentives (defined as the share of retained revenue) faced by provincial governments have grown increasingly stronger as a result of the decentralization started in the 1980s: the correlation between ex post (realized) provincial budgetary revenue collection and expenditure after decentralization reforms is about four times as high as before reforms. Second, higher ex ante fiscal incentives (measured by the contractual revenue retention rate of provincial governments) are found to have a positive effect on provincial growth performance. In other words, while fiscal decentralization per se would not lead to stronger growth, stronger fiscal incentives would do so. However, further empirical work would be needed to test the impact of the latest round of intergovernmental fiscal reforms implemented in 1994.

Contrasting these views is the *market-hampering school,* claiming that competition among local governments has resulted in antimarket behavior (see, for example, Findlay, Wu, and Watson, 1995; and Young, 2000a). Under the centrally planned system, prices were skewed to concentrate value added, and hence profits, in industry. The gradual pace of the reform process, with few segments of the economy freed of control at any time, has created incentives to seek opportunities in the remaining distortions, thereby generating new distortions, mainly in the form of interregional barriers to trade. On this basis, this strand of literature concludes that the transition to a market economy has resulted in the fragmentation of the domestic market, possibly hampering the reform process down the road and preventing China from reaping the benefits of a large unified internal market.

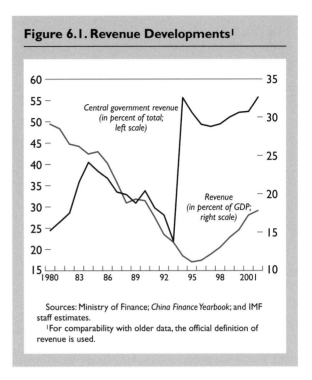

Figure 6.1. Revenue Developments[1]

Sources: Ministry of Finance; *China Finance Yearbook;* and IMF staff estimates.
[1]For comparability with older data, the official definition of revenue is used.

the share of the central government in total revenue—both had declined dramatically since the early 1980s, mainly due to weak tax administration capacity and lax control over local governments' collections (Figure 6.1) (Wong, 1997; and Ahmad, 1997). A new tax sharing system (TSS) was introduced, which shifted revenue collection and distribution away from a negotiated basis to a mix of tax assignments and tax sharing. A new value-added tax (VAT) was adopted,

to be shared between the center and the local governments. Revenue assigned to local governments included 25 percent of the new VAT, the business tax (a turnover tax), the personal income tax, and the enterprise income tax (EIT) levied on local state-owned enterprises (SOEs) and foreign-financed enterprises. The central government received 75 percent of the VAT, consumption taxes (excises) and trade-related taxes, and EIT from central SOEs (see also OECD, 2002a; and Ahmad and others, 2002 and 2004). The State Tax Administration was made responsible for the collection of central and shared taxes, while local government agencies were in charge of collecting local taxes. However, tax authority remained solely vested with the central government, as local governments had only limited powers to set rates for a few local taxes. These arrangements are still broadly applied, as no major changes have been introduced since 1994.[2]

From the perspective of raising revenue and increasing the share of revenue accruing to the center, the 1994 reform has been successful: revenues have quickly recovered from the trough in the mid-

---

[2]The 2002 budget introduced a new sharing formula for personal and corporate income taxes. According to the new formula, all proceeds from these taxes above the 2001 level are shared between the center and the provinces on the basis of a 50:50 ratio (changed to 60:40 in 2003). The share of these increased revenues received by the center is to be used for transfers to poorer provinces.

Table 6.2. Differences in Revenue Performance by Province, 1995 and 2002[1]

(In percent of provincial GDP)

	1995	2002	Change from 1995 to 2002
Top two provinces			
Beijing	15.1	23.4	8.3
Shanghai	16.9	22.4	5.5
Bottom two provinces			
Tibet	5.3	6.1	0.8
Henan	7.5	7.9	0.4
Unweighted average[2]	10.2	11.8	1.6

Source: *China Finance Yearbook, 2003.*
[1]Province refers to the first tier of subnational governments.
[2]Includes all provinces.

1990s, and the center's share has surged to above 55 percent—more than twice the level registered just before the reform (see Figure 6.1). However, important differences in revenue-generating capacity across provinces remain, and these have increased over time. For example, not only did Beijing raise almost four times the amount of revenue, as a share of GDP, than Henan in 2002, but the latter's revenue had remained virtually flat since 1995, while the former's had grown by more than 8 percent of GDP (Table 6.2).

The reason for this disparity lies mainly in the structure of the taxes assigned to local governments, which tends to favor richer provinces. As explained above, local tax revenues derive mainly from shared VAT, business taxes, and EIT (together accounting for about 70 percent of total local governments' revenue). The bases for these taxes typically cover the secondary (manufacturing) and tertiary (services) sectors; hence, coastal regions—where the share of GDP of secondary and tertiary industries is relatively high—benefit from the current fiscal system more than central and western provinces, whose economic structure relies heavily on the primary sector (agriculture-related taxes account for only 6 percent of local government taxes). A similar pattern applies to the personal income tax, whose yields are higher the larger the average household income—again, richer coastal provinces are favored.

Broadened Expenditure Mandates

The "recentralization" of revenue has not been accompanied by a reduction in expenditure assign-

ments. To the contrary, expenditure pressures on subnational governments have intensified, especially when measured relative to their own resources. While local governments' share of total expenditure has remained quite stable at around 70 percent during the last decade, local governments' expenditure has nonetheless become increasingly burdensome relative to local governments' own resources. For example, the ratio of local governments' expenditure to their own revenue has surged from about 103 percent in 1991 to about 180 percent in 2002. With an appropriate system of central transfers, there would be no financing gap, but the transfer system suffers from a number of drawbacks (see below). In addition, local governments' expenditure shares are above 90 percent in a number of areas (Table 6.3).

Various factors explain the proliferation of local governments' expenditure responsibilities. The industrial restructuring process has transferred previous spending responsibilities of SOEs—especially in social areas, such as education and health—to subnational governments as SOEs are reformed; increased and fast urbanization has created a need for subnational governments to provide basic infrastructure services (such as electricity and transportation); and the administration of pensions remains largely decentralized, in most cases all the way down to the county level, where there are signs of difficulties in paying pensions. In addition, minimum service standards set by the center create challenges for poorer counties, while richer subnational governments do not seem to experience similar difficulties. For example, the provision of healthcare services in rural areas—to be partly covered by specially-designed central subsidies—requires matching funds from receiving counties, further stretching their service provision capacity.

Inadequate Transfers

In addition to a clear redefinition of the tax assignments, the 1994 reform also redesigned the transfer system, moving away from ad hoc negotiated transfers toward a more rules-based and transparent mechanism. The transfer system is based on four main pillars.
- *Revenue returned* provides each province with 30 percent of the increase in VAT receipts and excise tax collection over the 1993 base (the year before the reform).
- *Specific-purpose grants* are earmarked transfers allocated on an ad hoc basis.
- *Subsidy transfers* or general-purpose grants help ensure that each province has adequate resources. They are rules-based and depend on variables such as provincial GDP, student-

Table 6.3. Shares of Central and Local Governments in Selected Budgetary Expenditure, 2001

	Shares of Total Expenditure (In percent)	Share of Center (In percent of item)	Share of Local Government (In percent of item)
Total	100.0	30.5	69.5
Of which:			
Culture, education, science, and health	17.8	10.8	89.2
Education	11.7	7.8	92.2
Health	3.0	2.2	97.8
Capital construction	13.4	34.3	65.7
National defense	7.7	99.2	0.8
Administration	6.4	2.7	97.3
Technical updates, transformation, and science	5.2	25.0	75.0
Tax administration	5.0	35.1	64.9
Agriculture	4.8	10.9	89.1
Policy subsidies	3.9	40.3	59.7
Urban maintenance and construction	3.4	0.0	100.0
Pension for retired employees	3.2	9.1	90.9
Armed police	1.2	92.3	7.7

Sources: Ministry of Finance data. Local expenditures include earmarked transfers from the central government.

teacher ratios, number of civil servants, and population density.
• *Fixed subsidies* ensure that every province has total revenues no lower than subsidies in 1993.
Ahmad and others (2004) provide a snapshot of these transfers (Table 6.4). Central transfers are sizable, representing about 44 percent of total local

government's resources and financing 48 percent of local governments' expenditure in 2002 (World Bank, 2002 and 2003). Despite their large size, transfers have nonetheless proved inadequate to provide sufficient financial support to the provision of essential services such as rural education and rural public health. The predominance of "transfers" under the

Table 6.4. Transfers from the Central to Local Governments

	1997	1998	1999	2000	2001
	(In percent of GDP)				
Revenue returned	2.7	2.7	2.6	2.6	2.3
Specific-purpose transfers	0.7	1.1	1.7	1.6	2.0
General-purpose transfers[1]	0.3	0.3	0.5	0.9	1.4
Fixed subsidies under old system	0.2	0.1	0.1	0.1	0.1
Total	3.8	4.2	5.0	5.2	5.8
	(In percent of total transfers)				
Revenue returned	70.5	62.7	53.0	48.9	38.9
Specific-purpose transfers	18.1	26.4	33.8	30.6	34.6
General-purpose transfers[1]	7.5	7.5	10.2	17.9	24.5
Fixed subsidies under old system	3.9	3.4	2.9	2.7	2.0
Total	100.0	100.0	100.0	100.0	100.0

Sources: Chinese authorities; IMF staff estimates; and Ahmad and others (2004).
[1]Include transfers for income equalization.

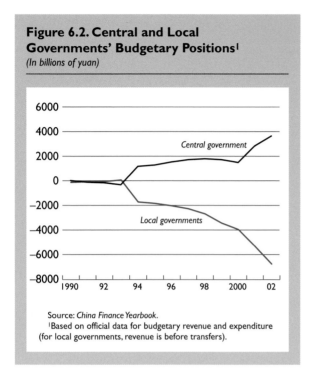

Figure 6.2. Central and Local Governments' Budgetary Positions[1]
(In billions of yuan)

Source: *China Finance Yearbook.*
[1]Based on official data for budgetary revenue and expenditure (for local governments, revenue is before transfers).

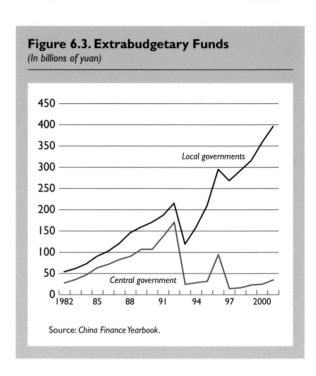

Figure 6.3. Extrabudgetary Funds
(In billions of yuan)

Source: *China Finance Yearbook.*

revenue returned principle makes the current system implicitly regressive, as richer provinces receive most transfers. Although declining, these transfers still represent about 40 percent of total transfers from the center to the provinces. In contrast, general-purpose transfers (including transfers for income equalization), although growing, represent only a quarter of the total. The system's ability to redistribute fiscal revenues across provinces therefore remains limited.

Specific-purpose grants comprise hundreds of different earmarked grants, allocated on an ad hoc negotiated basis. Their increasing share reflects the proactive regional policy that the center is carrying out. However, by their nature these grants make the transfer system less transparent and more difficult to monitor, as the center lacks the ability to track how the related funds are effectively spent; they also undermine the rules-based character of the transfer system that the 1994 reform aimed to introduce. Ongoing reforms to create a treasury system should assist in improving the transparency and control of expenditure at all levels of government. Finally, fixed subsidies, introduced to guarantee that every province maintained revenue no lower than the 1993 level, are progressively becoming less relevant and are gradually being phased out.

Uncertainty about the size and timing of central transfers further complicates budgetary formulation and execution at the local government level. Where local governments do not have sufficient resources of

their own to carry out important public functions, either expenditure cuts are effected elsewhere, arrears accumulate, or local governments attempt to raise funds outside the budget system.

Some Implications of the Current System

The imbalance between increased expenditure by subnational governments and their budgetary revenue has widened over time, resulting in a sharp deterioration of their fiscal position (before transfers) since 1994 (Figure 6.2). Such vertical imbalances are not uncommon in large federations (for example, Australia and India), as they allow the center to play a bigger role in macroeconomic stabilization and equalization. In China, however, the large share of revenue returned in total transfers limits the amount of unencumbered resources available to the center for redistribution and works against the principle of equalization (Ahmad and others, 2004).

Faced with intensifying financial pressures—resulting from limited tax setting powers, an inadequate transfer system, and a legal prohibition to borrow—local governments have continued to raise revenue outside the budget system, mainly in the form of fees and charges that accrue to locally managed extrabudgetary funds. While reported extrabudgetary funds managed by the central government

---

Box 6.2. Fiscal Risks of Local Governments: The 2002 Audit Report[1]

The Chinese authorities are aware of possible fiscal risks generated at the local government level. This box summarizes some key findings of the 2002 Audit Report, which illustrates some cases of such fiscal risks and identifies the underlying causes for their buildup.

Misuse of Government Loans

Some local projects financed by loans from the central government are plagued by loss, waste, and ineffective utilization of funds. For example, 37 sewage treatment projects costed at about RMB 6 billion received about RMB 2 billion in government loans. But, owing to inadequate planning, failure to provide counterpart funding, and insufficient operating funds, construction was not finished (or, in some cases, not even begun) on 15 projects; seven of 16 completed projects failed to meet design specifications, and the completion of supporting facilities frequently lagged behind the main projects, with the result that equipment lay idle and the programs failed to produce their planned overall effect.

The audit of projects involving 18 major airports and 38 secondary-route airports revealed that many of the airports had suffered huge losses and that their operations were in financial difficulty. Nine of 12 major completed airports were losing money, with the combined loss amounting to RMB 1.4 billion. Thirty-seven of the 38 secondary-route airports had also lost money, with

a combined loss of RMB 1.5 billion in 2000–2001. In 2001, the passenger turnaround capacity of 38 secondary-route airports was only a quarter of that estimated in feasibility studies, and the Mianzhou airport achieved only 3 percent of its design capacity.

Insufficient Funding from the Center and Increasing Arrears

At the end of 2001, 49 cities and counties had a total of RMB 1.6 billion in debt, equivalent to 2.1 times their disposable financial resources for that year. In some cases, accumulated arrears kept on growing. As of September 2002, 42 counties and townships had RMB 1.8 billion in wage arrears—more than three times the arrears in 1998.

Underlying Reasons

The Audit Report also identifies some causes of these problems:

- Lack of stable revenue sources at the subnational level. Currently, counties and townships rely on transfers from higher government levels for 60 percent of their expenditures. However, many earmarked subsidies require counterpart funds, which increases the fiscal pressure on these local governments.
- "Improper attitudes toward fiscal management," which induce local governments to "blindly set up projects and even create *image projects.*"
- Excessively rapid growth in the numbers of persons supported by public funds (unfunded mandates). Since 1994, while the total population of counties and townships has increased by 4.6 percent, the number of people supported by public funds has increased by 22 percent.

---

[1]The Audit Report is produced annually by the National Audit Office of the People's Republic of China (CNAO), the official institution in charge of auditing government finances. The CNAO is required by the Constitution to report its findings to the State Council.

---

declined significantly after the 1994 reform, those controlled by subnational governments have continued to increase (Figure 6.3).[3]

Financing constraints have also induced subnational governments to seek ways to circumvent their legal funding limits by creating channels for raising indirect financing and shifting some public functions to seemingly "nongovernment" entities. Large-scale infrastructure projects offer an example: in most provinces, there has been intense activity to build highways, airports, and urban ring roads. Most of these projects have been financed by bank loans, on the expectation that the sales of appreciated land

leases in the areas where these projects are implemented will make the latter financially viable. However, these projects may also represent significant fiscal risks in case local governments, and ultimately the central government, are called upon to shoulder the associated fiscal costs. The shift of public functions to nongovernment entities to overcome legal borrowing constraints might also generate opportunities for waste and corruption, without necessarily improving effective service delivery. The authorities are aware of these problems, as candidly described in the 2002 Audit Report (Box 6.2).

Conclusions

The 1994 reform of the structure of intergovernmental fiscal relations has been successful in a number of areas: it has streamlined the tax system and

---

[3]A provincial pilot project, launched in 2001, aims to replace the numerous fees with a surcharge on the local agricultural tax. This so-called tax-for-fees reform is to be gradually extended to all provinces.

enhanced tax administration, boosted revenue, and increased budgetary resources available to the center. However, there are growing signs that the transfer system, whose aim was to compensate local governments for revenue lost to the center and promote equalization across regions, is in need of reform; in particular, it has proven inadequate to address the large regional income disparities. Local governments' expenditure mandates remain unclear and, in some cases, largely unfunded; pension costs are a case in point, where local governments are ill-equipped to shoulder the related costs and higher-level pooling is called for. Finally, indirect means of local government financing and creation of implicit liabilities at the local level may represent significant fiscal risks, underscoring the need for a comprehensive and centralized monitoring of subnational operations. These challenges will need to be addressed early on, not only to reduce regional disparities but, most importantly, to prevent erosion of social cohesion and weakening of public support for future reforms.

VII Banking Sector Developments

Steven Barnett

An effective banking sector is essential for promoting financial intermediation and the efficient allocation of resources. In China, this is especially true given the high saving and investment rates, and the central role of banks in financial intermediation. Indeed, banks are the dominant players in the Chinese financial sector. Banks carry out most financial intermediation as the stock and bond markets are still relatively small. In 2003, for example, the increase in domestic and foreign currency loans made by financial institutions was RMB 3 trillion (26 percent of GDP), compared with funds raised through the stock markets totaling RMB 136 billion (1 percent of GDP) and corporate bond issuance of only RMB 36 billion (0.3 percent of GDP). Similarly, at the end of 2003, the stock of bank loans stood at 145 percent of GDP, while the total stock market capitalization of the Shenzen and Shanghai stock markets was only 37 percent of GDP.

In parallel with the economy, the banking system in China, which is dominated by state-owned banks, has been undergoing a transition toward market principles. But the legacy of policy lending has resulted in these banks being burdened by a large stock of nonperforming loans (NPLs). Substantial progress has been made in recent years in improving the financial position and market orientation of state banks, but many challenges remain. China's continuing integration with the global economy, capital account liberalization, and opening up of the banking system to foreign competition under the WTO accession agreement underscore the importance of pushing ahead with the ongoing reforms.

This section describes the present structure of the banking system and examines recent developments in banking aggregates, analyzes some of the main challenges and risks facing the system, and describes the reforms that are under way to meet some of these challenges.

The Banking System Today

The main features of the banking system are that it is predominantly state owned, is very large, and is growing fast. An international comparison illustrates

Figure 7.1. Selected Economies: Ratio of Domestic Credit to GDP

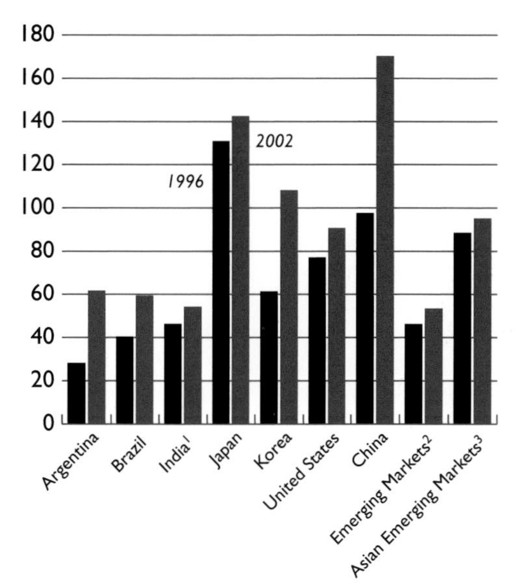

Source: IMF, *International Financial Statistics.*
[1] Refers to 2001 for India.
[2] Average for the group of countries used for the calculation of the EMBI+ index, that is, Argentina, Brazil, Bulgaria, Colombia, Ecuador, Egypt, Korea, Malaysia, Mexico, Morocco, Nigeria, Panama, Peru, the Philippines, Poland, Qatar, Russia, South Africa, Turkey, Ukraine, and Venezuela.
[3] Average for the following economies: Hong Kong SAR, Indonesia, Korea, Malaysia, the Philippines, Singapore, and Thailand.

these latter two points, as the ratio of credit to GDP is among the highest across a broad sample of economies and has also grown quite substantially since the mid-1990s (Figure 7.1).

Market Structure

Government entities of one form or another are still the main owners of the banks. The banking system (deposit money banks) includes the four wholly state-owned commercial banks (SCBs)—the Agri-

43

Table 7.1. Deposit Money Banks' Market Shares
(In percent of total)

	Total Assets		Credit[1]		Deposits	
	March 2002	Sept. 2003	March 2002	Sept. 2003	March 2002	Sept. 2003
State commercial banks	65.0	62.3	62.7	61.2	68.3	64.9
Joint-stock commercial banks	12.5	15.0	11.6	14.9	12.0	14.7
Rural credit cooperatives	10.2	10.4	11.6	11.3	12.3	11.8
Foreign-funded banks	1.5	1.3	1.2	1.0	0.4	0.4
Other	10.8	10.9	13.0	11.6	7.0	8.1
Memorandum Item:						
Specific depository institutions						
(in percent of deposit money banks)[2]	7.4	7.0	8.7	8.6	1.2	1.0

Source: CEIC database.

[1]Defined as claims on the nonfinancial sector, claims on other sectors, or domestic credit.

[2]Specific depository institutions as a share of deposit money bank total.

cultural Bank of China (ABC), Bank of China (BOC), China Construction Bank (CCB), and Industrial and Commercial Bank of China (ICBC); other commercial banks, also known as joint-stock commercial banks (JSCBs), which have more diverse ownership structures that may include subnational governments as well as domestic or foreign private investors (as of December 2003, there were 11 JSCBs); rural credit cooperatives (RCCs) that focus on rural lending; and several types of smaller institutions.[1] In addition to the deposit money banks, there are also some specific depository institutions, which, for example, include the China Development Bank and China Export & Import Bank, but as a group their total assets are less than 10 percent of those at deposit money banks. The two banks mentioned above, along with the Agricultural Development Bank of China, are classified as policy banks and have a more explicit focus on development objectives.

China's banking system is by most measures quite large. This is a reflection of the predominant role of banks in financial intermediation, the size of the economy, high household saving rates, and capital account restrictions that limit overseas investment opportunities. Financial institutions' renminbi loans and deposits amounted to 136 percent and 178 percent of GDP, respectively, at the end of 2003. Total assets at deposit money banks amounted to over 200 percent of GDP (around $3 trillion). This figure is comparable to the size of the banking system relative to GDP in industrial countries, and well above most countries at comparable per capita income levels (Karacadag, 2003). In terms of asset size, the four SCBs were among the top 40 banks globally and were the largest four in Asia, excluding Japan (*Banker,* 2003).

The SCBs are by far the largest banks, although JSCBs have recently been gaining market share. The four SCBs together account for more than 60 percent of total assets, claims on the nonfinancial sector, and deposits (Table 7.1). Since March 2002, however, these shares have been falling, with JSCBs gaining roughly an equal amount. For example, in terms of deposits, JSCBs have gained and SCBs have lost around 3 percentage points in market share since March 2002.[2] Next in terms of size are the RCCs, which have held steady at slightly above 10 percent of the market. All other deposit money banks combined account for less than 15 percent of the market by any of the above criteria. Foreign-funded banks, in particular, have only a small share, accounting for less than 1½ percent of the market by any of these measures.

Recent Trends

Both loans and deposits have been growing rapidly over the past few years. The stock of renminbi loans at financial institutions grew by 17 percent in 2002 and by 21 percent in 2003 (Figure 7.2).

---

[1]These include urban commercial banks, rural commercial banks, foreign-funded banks, urban credit cooperatives, finance companies, and the Agricultural Development Bank of China.

[2]Due to breaks in the series, these figures are not comparable with earlier data. Karacadag (2003) reviews earlier developments, which show a similar trend.

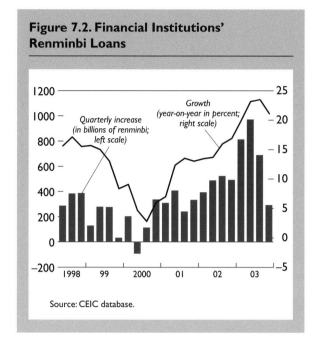

**Figure 7.2. Financial Institutions'
Renminbi Loans**

Growth
(year-on-year in percent;
right scale)

Quarterly increase
(in billions of renminbi;
left scale)

Source: CEIC database.

medium- and long-term lending (loans greater than one-year maturity) to roughly 40 percent by the end of 2003. Other types of loans that do not fit in either category—for example, trust loans, discount bills, or financial leasing—have been increasing fairly rapidly in the last two years.

Finally, as for the allocation of credit, consumer credit accounts for a fairly small but growing share of renminbi loans. Consumer loans grew by nearly 50 percent in 2003, which pushed up the share of consumer loans in total renminbi loans from 8 percent in 2002 to 10 percent in 2003. Most consumer loans are for individual housing, which, as of the end of 2003, accounted for three-fourths of consumer lending.

Challenges and Risks

Developments in the banking system have significant macroeconomic and fiscal implications. As argued above, banks in China play a crucial role as the primary domestic financial intermediaries. A healthy and well-functioning banking system is, therefore, important for promoting macroeconomic stability. At the same time, strengthening the banking system is also key for minimizing the prospective fiscal cost of bank restructuring (see Section V), which is largely related to the high NPL ratios. The state is still the primary owner of most banks, and, notwithstanding the lack of explicit deposit insurance, there is an implicit deposit guarantee given the importance of confidence in the banking system for macroeconomic and social stability.

In this regard, the main challenges for the banks are to improve their commercial orientation and strengthen their financial position. These challenges are interrelated, as improving the commercial orientation of the banks is a key step toward improving their financial health, both by reducing future accumulation of NPLs and boosting profitability. In turn, this would help redress the balance sheet weaknesses of the banks, and thereby directly lower the contingent fiscal liability. In addition, enhanced corporate governance and risk management practices would allow banks to better perform their intermediary roles, which would promote a more efficient allocation of resources.

Meanwhile, deposits also grew rapidly, with the system-wide loan to deposit ratio having fallen slightly to just over 75 percent at the end of 2003.[3] Consistent with their growing market share, credit growth has been especially rapid in the JSCBs. For example, from Q1:2002 to Q3:2003, claims on non-financial institutions increased by 72 percent in JSCBs compared to 31 percent at SCBs.

The banks still predominately operate in local currency. Foreign currency loans have accounted for roughly 6 percent of all loans, a figure that has been fairly steady for the past few years. In 2003, however, foreign currency loans grew by more than 25 percent, somewhat faster than the growth in renminbi loans. Foreign currency deposits, in contrast, declined by 2 percent during the first three quarters of 2003. Concomitantly, the share of foreign currency deposits in total deposits has also declined to 6 percent, compared with 8 percent in March 2002 (when data are first available). Recent developments in foreign currency lending and deposits probably reflect, at least in part, expectations of a renminbi appreciation.

Regarding the maturity structure of RMB loans, most loans are still short term although their share has been declining. Since 1997, the share of short-term loans has fallen from three-fourths of all loans to around one-half, with a nearly concomitant rise in

History

The challenges facing the banks should, however, be understood in a historical context. The banks, especially the SCBs, primarily focused on allocating credit to SOEs based on government plans rather than commercially-based lending decisions. Many of these SOEs are now unable to repay the loans, con-

---

[3]The regulatory prudential limit is 75 percent. However, the definition of financial institutions includes some institutions, such as the policy banks, that are not subject to the prudential limit.

Table 7.2. Reported Nonperforming Loans

| | In Billions of Renminbi | | Nonperforming Loans | | | |
| | | | In percent of total loans | | In percent of GDP | |
	2002	2003	2002	2003	2002	2003
Four-tier classification						
Financial institutions in banking sector	2,557	2,400	20	15	25	21
SCBs	1,721	1,590	22	17	17	14
JSCBs	162	154	10	7	2	1
RCCs	513	505	37	30	5	4
City commercial banks	105	99	18	13	1	1
Others	57	52	...	...	1	0
Five-tier classification						
SCBs	2,088	1,917	26	20	20	16
JSCBs	203	188	12	8	2	2
Policy banks	341	336	20	17	3	3

Sources: China Banking Regulatory Commission.

tributing to the banks' high NPL ratios, low profitability, and weak financial positions. In addition, the banks' operations, procedures, and organizational structures were also geared to their historical roles and are still in the process of being modernized to meet international standards. Thus, the challenges facing the banks are in large part a historical legacy and an integral part of the broader economic transition toward a more market-based economy.

Due in part to their differing historical roles, the degree of financial strength varies across the types of banks. The JSCBs are generally considered to be the strongest, reflecting the fact that they are fairly new and, thus, less burdened with historical problems; moreover, some are also publicly listed or have some private ownership, factors that tend to contribute to sounder governance. The RCCs face significant challenges, which are in part related to their small size and their focus on generally small-scale agricultural lending. The SCBs bear the largest imprint of their historical roles, as they were the main banks used in allocating credit under central planning. Their loan portfolios, customer relationships, and operations were geared to their particular roles, which was primarily lending to SOEs.

The government took steps in the late 1990s to significantly strengthen the financial position of the SCBs. In 1998, it injected capital of RMB 270 billion (about 3½ percent of GDP) into the four SCBs. And, in 1999–2000, four asset management companies (AMCs) were created that purchased RMB 1.4 trillion, or 14 percent of GDP, in NPLs from the SCBs and the China Development Bank. The NPLs were purchased at book value, and, in return, the

AMCs issued bonds to the SCBs, thereby substantially strengthening the banks' financial positions. Subsequently, however, some AMCs have not always been servicing these bonds on a timely basis, suggesting that these bonds may to some degree have to be regarded as nonperforming assets (although not as NPLs).

Capital Adequacy Ratios, Nonperforming Loans, and Provisioning

The banks' balance sheet shortcomings are manifested, to varying degrees, in a combination of high NPLs, low capital adequacy ratios (CARs), and underprovisioning. These concepts are all interrelated. For example, the large stock of NPLs creates a need for provisioning for potential loan losses, but provisioning reduces profitability and thereby effectively lowers capital (and the CAR). Viewed more simply, the high NPLs provide an indication of the health of the banks and, thus, the potential fiscal costs. At the same time, CARs in China do not always provide a meaningful indication of bank soundness, as they would fall—by a potentially large amount—if banks were to provision in line with international norms.

Recently, there has been significant progress in reducing reported NPL ratios, but they nonetheless remain high. Under China's four-tier classification system—which is based primarily on the aging of loans and only counts the overdue portion of loans as nonperforming—the NPL ratio at the end of 2003 was 15 percent, down 5 percentage points from 2002 (Table 7.2). While the growth in loans—that is, the increase in the denominator of the NPL ratio—clearly helped in reducing this ratio, there was also a decline in absolute terms of RMB 160 billion (1½ percent of GDP) in the stock of NPLs. The ratio of NPLs to GDP declined from 25 percent in 2002 to 21 percent in 2003. Much of this improvement in the overall NPL position is attributable to declining NPLs among the SCBs. The RCCs have the highest NPL ratios, and account for 20 percent of system-wide NPLs (compared with their 10 percent market share). The JSCBs have the lowest NPL ratio at 7 percent.

The SCBs and JSCBs have also succeeded in migrating to a five-tier classification system, broadly in line with international standards. Under this classification, NPLs are higher, by around 20 percent or more, relative to the four-tier classification. The five-tier classification results in higher reported NPLs because the entire amount of an overdue loan is classified as an NPL, whereas the four-tier classification only counted the overdue portion (that is, the missed principal payments) as an NPL. At the end of 2003, the average NPL ratios using the five-tier classification stood at 20 percent for the SCBs and 8 percent for the JSCBs. These data corroborate the main findings from the four-tier classification—specifically, that both the NPL ratios and the absolute amount of NPLs have declined. Moreover, this continues the good progress that the SCBs have been making in reducing NPLs over the past few years (Box 7.1).

Beyond NPLs, the banks also have other nonperforming assets on their books. Nonperforming assets include NPLs as well as noncredit assets that are not performing, such as foreclosed collateral, and are thus by definition larger than NPLs. In addition, much of the outstanding NPLs that were transferred to the AMCs have not yet been resolved. As of September 2003, the AMCs had disposed of 30 percent of the stock of NPLs that they had originally assumed, which had a face value of RMB 1.4 trillion. Of these disposals, the total and cash recovery rates (relative to face value) were, respectively, 31 percent and 21 percent.

As noted above, the CARs in China should be interpreted carefully given the large amount of NPLs that are not adequately provisioned for. As highlighted in Box 7.1, the CARs of the SCBs would fall substantially if the banks provisioned according to the rules that will take effect in 2005. At the end of 2003, the average CAR for JSCBs was 7.4 percent, and the average for the city commercial banks was 6.1 percent. It should also be noted that claims on SOEs were given a smaller risk weight than suggested by international norms, which also boosts reported CARs. Finally, given the huge number of branches and the magnitude of changes being implemented at the banks—including the new five-tier

classification system—there is a possibility that the reported NPL numbers could be further refined.

Recent Reforms

China has made significant progress in improving the strength and institutional setting of the financial sector over the last decade (see Karacadag, 2003). Many of these reforms aim to further break away from the historical legacies of the state-controlled credit system and move the orientation of the banks toward one that is governed by commercial principles. Recent policy announcements, including the communiqué from the Third Plenum of the Sixteenth Central Committee of the Communist Party of China, have also highlighted the importance that the authorities attach to moving forward with banking system reform. The commitment to open the banking system to foreign competition as part of China's World Trade Organization accession agreement provides a further impetus for pushing ahead expeditiously with the reform process.[4]

Institutional Reforms

Institutional reforms have been implemented aimed at creating a competitive and modern banking environment, including one that is well regulated and open to foreign participation.

The China Banking Regulatory Commission (CBRC) was established in April 2003 to take over the supervisory and regulatory responsibilities for banks from the People's Bank of China (PBC). The motivation was to more clearly distinguish between monetary policy and bank supervision objectives; this would also allow the PBC to focus more on monetary policy, including an increased reliance on market-oriented instruments. The CBRC set as its near-term priorities the reduction of NPLs, quicker reform of the SCBs, and reform of the rural financial system (especially the RCCs). Among other initiatives, the CBRC required that all SCBs and JSCBs adopt the five-tier loan classification system beginning in 2004—publicly listed banks had already been required to use it. More generally, the authorities have emphasized the importance of improving internal management, risk control, and governance of the banks while at the same time strengthening the supervisory and regulatory framework.

As a complement to the above institutional changes, the market is also being opened up to for-

---

[4]China's commitments call for opening up of the banking sector to foreign financial institutions five years after accession (which occurred on December 11, 2001).

Box 7.1. Developments in State Commercial Banks

Evaluating the financial performance of the four state commercial banks (SCBs) illustrates the progress that has been made in strengthening their financial positions, and also points to some of the challenges that will need to be addressed by future reforms.

NPLs. The SCBs have made substantial progress in reducing their NPL ratios (see table below), yet the ratios remain high by international standards. While growth in the stock of loans—that is, the denominator of the NPL ratio—has contributed to this decline, there has also been an absolute reduction in NPLs; for the four SCBs combined, the stock of NPLs declined by RMB 170 billion in 2003 to RMB 1.9 trillion (with the NPL ratio falling from 26 percent to 20 percent).

Special mention loans. In addition to NPLs, the banks also have a substantial amount of special mention loans, which are considered performing loans but have a higher risk of becoming nonperforming in the future. At the end of 2002, the share of special mention loans was 14 percent for BOC, 19 percent for CCB, and 12 percent for ICBC.

Provisioning. A substantial increase in provisioning would have been required to meet the CBRC's 2005 requirements. These requirements call for general provisions of 1 percent of all loans and specific provisions of 2 percent of special mention loans, 20–30 percent of substandard loans, 40–60 percent of doubtful loans, and 100 percent of loss loans. The table quantifies the increase in provisioning that would have been required at the end of 2002 for the SCBs to have met these requirements.

CARs. At the end of 2002, only BOC met the 8 percent CAR threshold, which is considered the international minimum standard and is the minimum called for by China's existing laws and regulations (although there has been substantial regulatory forbearance in this regard). Moreover, if the banks provisioned in line with the 2005 rules, the CARs would be much lower.

Profitability. The SCBs' profitability, as measured by international standards, is fairly low. Of note, in this regard, the 4 SCBs were in the top 40 banks in the world in terms of asset size, but none ranked higher than 700 (out of 1,000) in terms of return on assets (*Banker,* 2003). Nevertheless, all four of the SCBs recorded positive net profits in both 2001 and 2002.

Taxes. Notwithstanding their low profits, the banks are heavily taxed. Total taxes as a share of adjusted profit (i.e., total taxes divided by the sum of net profit plus total taxes) was greater than 50 percent for ABC, CCB, and ICBC in both 2001 and 2002. For BOC it was slightly lower, but still above 40 percent in both years. Moreover, ABC, CCB, and ICBC paid very little income tax with the business tax accounting for virtually their entire tax bill.

The 2003 balance sheets for BOC and CCB, however, should look substantially stronger. Each received a \$22.5 billion (equivalent to RMB 186 billion) capital injection at the end of 2003. In addition, most of the SCBs have reported further increases in operating profits, which should provide scope to further strengthen their balance sheets.

Performance of the SCBs

| | NPL Ratio (In percent of total loans)[1] | | | | 2002 CAR[2] | | Additional Provisioning[3] | | | |
| | | | | | | | In billions of renminbi | | Percent of capital | |
	2000	2001	2002	2003	Total	Core	Low	High	Low	High
ABC	...	42	37	...	...	...	...	...	...	...
BOC	27	28	22	16	8.2	7.9	196	233	104	124
CCB	21	19	15	9	6.9	5.8	122	156	95	122
ICBC	34	30	26	21	5.5	5.5	415	518	261	326

Sources: Bank annual statements; China Banking Regulatory Commission; and IMF staff calculations.

[1]Data for 2003 are based on preliminary information.

[2]Total or core (that is, tier 1) capital as a share of risk-weighted assets.

[3]Additional provisions needed to meet the 2005 provisioning standards using end of 2002 data. The low (high) estimates use 20 (30) percent and 40 (60) percent for substandard and doubtful loans, respectively.

---

eign participation. This should help improve the commercial orientation of the banks, both by promoting competition and facilitating the transfer of foreign technical expertise. As part of its WTO accession, China has committed to open the banking sector to foreign financial institutions by December

2006. In particular, the commitments specify that by this time all geographic restrictions limiting where foreign financial institutions may operate will be removed, any nonprudential restrictions (for example, on ownership or operation) will also be removed, and that foreign financial institutions will be allowed to provide services to all Chinese clients.

The WTO accession commitments also called for intermediate steps in some of these areas. Upon accession, there were already few restrictions on foreign currency business. Foreign financial institutions were allowed to conduct foreign currency business with all clients and with no geographic restrictions on their operations. Regarding renminbi business, effective December 2003 foreign financial institutions were allowed to operate in four more cities, bringing the total to 13, and conduct business with Chinese enterprises.[5] Previously, renminbi business was restricted to foreign enterprises and individuals, as well as citizens of Hong Kong SAR and Macao SAR. In addition to the commitments made under the WTO agreement, the capital requirements for foreign funded financial institutions were lowered, and the ceiling on equity that could be held by a single foreign investor was raised from 15 percent to 20 percent—the overall limit on equity held by all foreigners was, however, kept at 25 percent.

Specific Measures

Complementing the above institutional steps, several more specific measures have also been implemented recently, including capital injection, interest rate liberalization, and tax reform that should help strengthen the banking system. Notwithstanding the progress already made, there is scope for further reforms in each of these areas.

At the end of 2003, the State Council authorized the use of $45 billion of international reserves to boost the capital of BOC and CCB. The capital injection into BOC and CCB was an important step as part of a broader reform strategy for the SCBs. These two banks were chosen as pilots for the SCB reform, with the ultimate goal of finding a strategic investor and eventual public listing. As noted in Box 7.1, the capital injection will substantially improve the balance sheets of these banks and facilitate an acceleration of NPL resolution. The accompanying measures, however, are key for ensuring that the capital is used effectively and leads to improvements in the

banks' commercial orientation, transparency, and governance. These measures include upgrading internal management, improved auditing, more prudent provisioning, and closer supervisory oversight.

In order to operate on a real commercial basis, however, banks also need to have a degree of flexibility in setting lending and deposit interest rates. In this regard, the further liberalization of lending rates in December 2003 was an important step. The upper band on renminbi lending was raised and consolidated at 170 percent of the benchmark rate, while the lower band was kept at 90 percent.[6] The added flexibility will allow the banks to deepen their commercial orientation, including by better pricing risk, and at the same time reach out to new customers, especially small and medium-sized enterprises. Banks will, however, have to develop expertise in risk assessment in order to appropriately exploit their increased flexibility. There was no change in the policy on deposit rates, which, for renminbi deposits, generally must be set at the benchmark.[7]

Banks in China face a fairly heavy tax burden, which directly and indirectly impedes their ability to strengthen their balance sheets. The direct impact is that the tax burden reduces after-tax profit, thereby reducing the financial resources available to boost provisioning and CARs. Banks are subject to a 33 percent corporate income tax and a business tax that is levied on gross income. As illustrated in Box 7.1, SCBs faced a heavy average tax burden largely as a result of the business tax. There has, however, been some progress in lowering the tax burden for banks. The business tax was reduced by 1 percentage point to 5 percent in 2003, in what was the last of the scheduled annual reductions. In addition to the direct impact of the tax rates, the tax system also indirectly discourages banks from cleaning up their balance sheets. Banks are not allowed to deduct specific provisions from income for tax purposes, in contrast to standard international practice. This creates a disincentive for provisioning against NPLs and thereby discourages the banks' from cleaning up their balance sheets. Continued progress toward a modern and fair tax regime would help promote the commercial orientation of the banks and also allow them to strengthen their balance sheets by earning a reasonable profit.

---

[5]Jinan, Fuzhou, Chengdu, and Chongqing were added in December 2003 to the existing nine cites—Shanghai, Shenzen, Tianjin, Dalian, Guangzhou, Zhuhai, Qingdao, Nanjing, and Wuhan. Under China's commitments, Kunming, Beijing, and Xiamen are scheduled to be added by December 2004, followed by Shantou, Ningbo, Shenyang, and Xi'an by December 2005.

[6]Previously, the upper band varied by the type of borrower with the highest ceiling being 130 percent (applicable to small and medium-sized enterprises). After the reform, for example, with the benchmark rate at 5.31 percent for one-year loans as of December 2003, the acceptable range would be 4.78 percent to 9.03 percent. For RCCs, the upper band was raised from the previous ceiling of 150 percent to 200 percent of the benchmark rate.

[7]For example, as of December 2003, the benchmark rates were 0.72 percent for demand deposits and 1.71 percent for three-month time deposits.

Conclusions

Significant progress has been made in strengthening and modernizing China's banking system, but many important challenges still remain. Key areas of progress include improvements in the supervisory regime, including the establishment of the CBRC; the ongoing opening of the market to foreign financial institutions; expanded flexibility in setting lending interest rates; and the measures aimed at strengthening and modernizing SCBs, including the December 2003 capital injection into two of them. Bringing the institutional and regulatory frameworks up to international standards will be a key component of the reform process. Against this backdrop, the banks need to adjust to all of these changes and at the same time improve their balance sheets, modernize their operations, and prepare for the opening up of the market to international competition. Meeting these challenges will help ensure a well-functioning and healthy banking system that can promote macroeconomic stability and sustainable growth.

VIII Labor Market Performance and Prospects

Ray Brooks

China's labor market has undergone significant changes in the past twenty years. A more market-oriented labor market has emerged with the growing importance of the urban private sector, as state-owned enterprises (SOEs) are being downsized. At the same time, rural employment growth has slowed, and migrants have sought jobs in the dynamic coastal provinces. Overall employment growth has averaged just 1 percent since 1990, led mostly by urban job growth. Urban registered unemployment has risen in recent years to more than 4 percent, but alternative measures show a higher unemployment rate of 5 percent. In addition, a sizable surplus of labor still exists in the rural sector (about 150 million) and SOEs (about 10–11 million).

The main challenge facing China's labor market in the coming years will be to absorb the surplus labor into quality jobs while adjusting to World Trade Organization (WTO) accession. The analysis in this section suggests that, even if GDP growth averages 7 percent and the elasticity of nonagricultural employment growth to output growth is one-half (in line with historical experience), the unemployment rate could nonetheless double over the next three to four years to about 10 percent, before declining as SOE reform is completed. These pressures would be limited by stronger economic growth, especially in the private sector and the more labor-intensive service industries, which have generated the most jobs in recent years.

Against this background, this section first reviews the main trends in the Chinese labor market before outlining the progress on reforms. It then presents an analysis of the medium-term outlook for employment and unemployment, and discusses the main challenges that lie ahead.

Trends in China's Labor Market

China's population remains predominantly rural, despite a strong trend toward urbanization. Over 60 percent of the population was classified as rural by the 2000 census, compared with 80 percent two decades ago (Table 8.1).[1] While population growth slowed in the 1990s to average just under 1 percent a year, the labor force grew somewhat faster (about 1½ percent a year), owing to a rise in the working-age population. The labor force participation rate also rose to about 83 percent by the late 1990s. This is high by international standards because of the large proportion of rural workers in the labor force (two-thirds) and their very high participation rate.

Job growth since 1990 has taken place mainly in the urban areas. Overall job growth averaged just 1 percent since 1990, while jobs in urban areas increased at an average rate of 3 percent a year (or 6½ million a year) over the same period. Job growth in urban areas was achieved despite layoffs at SOEs equivalent to more than 10 percent of the urban labor force (Figure 8.1 and Table 8.2).[2,3] Employment in collectives also declined sharply from 1995 onward. The job losses at SOEs and collectives were more than offset by (1) job growth in the private sector (including foreign-funded enterprises), which created 25 million jobs during the period 1995–2002, and (2) an unexplained increase of 80 million jobs over the same period. The latter appears to be attributable in part to an increase in jobs in the informal sector (such as street vending, construction, and household services), which are not well covered by the establishment survey of the National Bureau of Statistics (NBS).[4]

---

[1]In part, the change reflects reclassification of some rural areas as urban.

[2]In the period 1998–2002, SOE employment was reduced by more than half to about 35 million. Some of these jobs were not lost, however, but simply reclassified as joint ownership firms for SOEs that were reorganized into shareholding units or formed partnerships with other entities. Separate data show layoffs of 24 million from SOEs and collectives during 1998–2002.

[3]Young (2000b) points out that employment numbers are not strictly comparable over time, particularly given that the 1990 census had a wider definition of employment than the old labor force survey. This resulted in a sharp jump in employment in 1990.

[4]In general, limitations in the labor market statistics make analysis of these data difficult. The aggregate labor market data are derived from the NBS labor force sample survey of almost 1 million persons, benchmarked to the 1990 and 2000 population censuses. The detail by industry sector is based on a separate

Table 8.1. Population, Labor Force, and Employment
(In millions, at end of year)

	1980	1990	1995	2000	2001	2002	2003 Est.
Population	987.1	1,143.3	1,211.2	1,265.8	1,276.3	1,284.5	1,292.3
Urban	191.4	301.9	351.7	458.4	480.6	502.1	...
Rural	795.7	841.4	859.5	807.4	795.6	782.4	...
Urban (percent of total)	19.4	26.4	29.0	36.2	37.7	39.1	...
Rural (percent of total)	80.6	73.6	71.0	63.8	62.3	60.9	...
Working age population (15–64)	594.1	763.1	829.0	888.0	894.3	903.0	...
Labor force[1]	429.0	653.2	687.4	739.9	744.3	753.6	...
Participation rate (in percent)[2]	72.2	85.6	82.9	83.3	83.2	83.5	...
Employment[3]	423.6	647.5	680.7	720.9	730.3	737.4	744.3
Employment growth			0.9	1.0	1.3	1.0	0.9
Unemployment[4]	5.4	5.7	6.7	19.1	14.1	16.2	...
In percent of total labor force	1.3	0.9	1.0	2.6	1.9	2.1	...
In percent of urban labor force	4.9	3.2	3.4	7.6	5.6	6.1	...
Urban							
Employment	105.3	170.4	190.4	231.5	239.4	247.8	256.4
Employment growth			2.1	3.3	3.4	3.5	3.5
Unemployment							
Registered	5.4	3.8	5.2	6.0	6.8	7.7	...
Laid-off workers (*xiagang*)[5]	...	...	...	9.1	7.4	6.2	...
Registered unemployed and *xiagang*	...	...	...	15.1	14.2	13.9	...
Unemployment rate (in percent)							
Registered	4.9	2.5	2.9	3.1	3.6	4.0	4.3
Registered unemployed and *xiagang*[6]	...	...	...	6.0	5.6	5.3	...
Rural							
Employment	318.4	477.1	490.3	489.3	490.9	489.6	487.9

Sources: *China Statistical Yearbook;* CEIC database; and author's estimates.

[1]From the labor force survey, defined as economically active persons 16 years and older, working either one hour or more in the reference week or looking for work.

[2]Labor force as percent of working age population. Data for the working age population defined consistently with the labor force (16 years and older) are not available.

[3]From the labor force survey, defined as those working for one hour or more in the reference week.

[4]Defined as difference between labor force and employment.

[5]Those *xiagang* remaining attached to remployment centers, at the end of the year.

[6]Calculated as percent of the urban labor force.

Most of the job growth in the past five to six years appears to have taken place in the service sector and in the coastal provinces. The pace of job creation was much faster in the tertiary sector than in other sectors (Table 8.3), and was concentrated in the coastal provinces (especially Fujian, Guangdong, Shandong, and Zhejiang). In those provinces, the private sector (and foreign direct investment) has

establishment survey that covers 2 million work units but excludes much of the private sector—hence, there is a large difference between aggregate employment and the sum of the parts, resulting in a sizable residual. See China's submission to the IMF's General Data Dissemination System at http://dsbb.imf.org for a description of the labor market data.

flourished since the government opened up special economic zones in the early 1980s. The development of the private sector was also helped by sound macroeconomic and structural policies that helped maintain strong economic growth (see Tseng and Rodlauer, 2003) and specific steps taken to foster the nonstate sector. These steps included formally elevating the private sector's role to parity with the state sector (in a 1999 amendment to the Constitution), continued external and domestic liberalization, and improved access to credit.

Urban registered unemployment has risen since the mid-1990s owing to job losses in the state sector. The registered unemployment rate, as measured by the Ministry of Labor and Social Services (MOLSS),

Figure 8.1. Employment and GDP

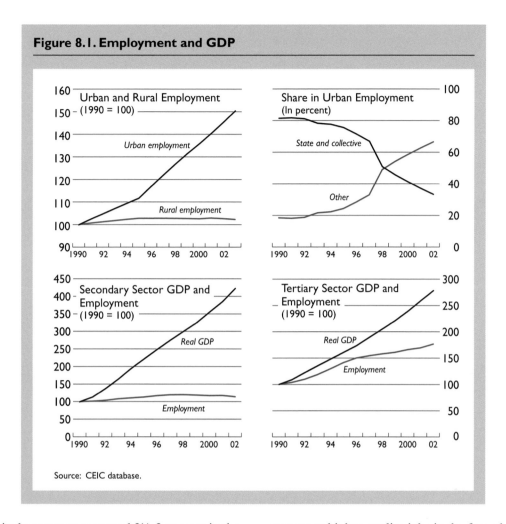

Source: CEIC database.

was relatively constant at around 2½–3 percent in the 1990s, but rose to 4 percent by 2002.[5]

Alternative measures show higher unemployment rates in recent years. Taking account of *xiagang* (laid-off workers), the total for registered unemployed and *xiagang* reached 5⅓ percent of the urban labor force by the end of 2002.[6] However, survey evidence suggests that a significant proportion of *xiagang* should not be classified as unemployed according to International Labor Organization (ILO) guidelines, as they work more than one hour a week in informal jobs.[7] Although informal sector workers may want higher-quality jobs in the formal sector or may want to work longer hours, they are not strictly considered as unemployed following ILO guidelines. Instead, they are considered to be underemployed.

In October 2002, the National Bureau of Statistics Commissioner stated that new estimates by the NBS suggested an urban unemployment rate (measured consistent with ILO guidelines) of about 4–5 percent of the labor force. The true level of unemployment, however, remains uncertain as it is not possible to accurately calculate the scale of the layoffs at state firms or of urban unemployment given the poor quality of the data (Solinger, 2002).

Urban unemployment varies considerably by region, with the highest rates in the northeastern provinces (see Brooks and Ran, 2003, for detailed data). At the end of 2002, the registered unemployment rate ranged from a low of 1.4 percent in Beijing to a high of 6.5 percent in the northeastern province of Heilongjiang. The regional variation is even greater for unemployment, including *xiagang,* with the northeastern region (or China's "rust-belt" con-

[5]The MOLSS measures unemployed persons as those in the age group from 16 to the age of retirement who are looking for work, have nonagricultural residence card (urban *hukou*), are able to work, want to work, and have registered in the local labor exchanges for work.

[6]*Xiagang* refers to workers laid off from SOEs who remain registered with reemployment centers.

[7]Zhao (2001) presents evidence of hidden reemployment from a 1999 survey of 6,500 *xiagang* and showed that about 60 percent of those still registered as laid-off workers were employed in the informal sector.

Table 8.2. Employment by Enterprise Ownership

	1980	1990	1995	2000	2001	2002	2003
	(In millions, at end of year)						
Total employment	423.6	647.5	680.7	720.9	730.3	737.4	744.3
Urban employment	105.3	170.4	190.4	231.5	239.4	247.8	256.4
State units	80.2	103.5	112.6	81.0	76.4	71.6	70.6[1]
Of which:							
SOEs	67.0	73.0	76.4	43.9	39.5	35.3	...
Institutions	22.0	21.6	26.1	26.4	26.2	25.8	...
Governments	4.7	8.9	10.1	10.7	10.7	10.5	...
Collective owned	24.3	35.5	31.5	15.0	12.9	11.2	10.8[1]
Jointly owned units[2]	0.0	1.0	3.7	13.4	15.2	18.3	...
Foreign funded[3]	0.0	0.7	5.1	6.4	6.7	7.6	...
Private units	0.8	6.7	20.6	34.0	36.6	42.7	...
Residual[4]	0.0	23.1	16.9	81.6	91.6	96.4	...
Rural employment	318.4	477.1	490.3	489.3	490.9	489.6	487.9
Town and village enterprises	30.0	92.7	128.6	128.2	130.9	132.9	...
Rural private owned	...	1.1	4.7	11.4	11.9	14.1	...
Self-employed	...	14.9	30.5	29.3	26.3	24.7	...
Farmers	288.4	368.4	326.4	320.4	321.8	317.9	...
	(In percent of total)						
Urban employment	100.0	100.0	100.0	100.0	100.0	100.0	100.0
State units	76.2	60.7	59.1	35.0	31.9	28.9	27.5
Of which:							
SOEs	63.7	42.8	40.1	19.0	16.5	14.2	...
Institutions	20.9	12.7	13.7	11.4	10.9	10.4	...
Governments	4.4	5.2	5.3	4.6	4.5	4.2	...
Collective owned	23.0	20.8	16.5	6.5	5.4	4.5	4.2
Jointly owned units[2]	...	0.6	1.9	5.8	6.4	7.4	...
Foreign funded[3]	0.0	0.4	2.7	2.8	2.8	3.1	...
Private units	0.8	3.9	10.8	14.7	15.3	17.2	...
Residual[4]	0.0	13.6	8.9	35.3	38.3	38.9	...
Rural employment	100.0	100.0	100.0	100.0	100.0	100.0	100.0
Town and village enterprises	9.4	19.4	26.2	26.2	26.7	27.1	...
Rural private owned	...	0.2	1.0	2.3	2.4	2.9	...
Self-employed	...	3.1	6.2	6.0	5.4	5.1	...
Farmers	90.6	77.2	66.6	65.5	65.6	64.9	...

Sources: *China Statistical Yearbook;* CEIC database; and author's estimates.
[1]September 2003.
[2]Jointly owned, limited corporations, and shareholding units.
[3]Includes Hong Kong SAR, Macao SAR, and Taiwan Province of China funded.
[4]The residual is the difference between the aggregate employment figure from the household survey and the detail by ownership from the establishment survey (which excludes much of the private sector).

centration of SOEs in declining industries) facing the largest unemployment pressures with a rate of almost 8 percent by the end of 2002—one and a half times the national average.

Rural employment growth was rapid in the late 1980s and early 1990s, as town and village enterprises (TVEs) evolved quickly to meet a pent-up demand for consumer goods and take advantage of a pool of cheap rural labor. By the mid-1990s, however, TVEs began to face financial problems brought on by poor management and growing competition from the private sector, and employment in these enterprises has declined slightly from a peak of 135 million in 1996. Most rural workers, however, are employed on farms. Growth of farm employment also rose sharply in the 1980s, putting added pressure on already small farm sizes, before declining by 20 million since 1990 as rural-to-urban migration picked up. Migrants have tended to move first to TVEs in rural areas, then further afield to the faster-growing eastern provinces (Cai, Dewen, and Yang, 2001). Migrants have been attracted to the Pearl

Table 8.3. Employment by Industry

	1980	1990	1995	2000	2001	2002
	(In millions, at end of year)					
Farming, forestry, animal husbandry, and fishery	291.2	341.8	330.2	333.6	329.7	324.9
Mining and quarrying	7.0	8.8	9.3	6.0	5.6	5.6
Manufacturing	59.0	86.2	98.0	80.4	80.8	83.1
Electricity, gas, and water	1.2	1.9	2.9	2.8	2.9	2.9
Construction	9.9	24.2	33.2	35.5	36.7	38.9
Geological prospecting and water conservancy	1.9	2.0	1.4	1.1	1.1	1.0
Transport, storage, and post and telecommunications	8.1	15.7	19.4	20.3	20.4	20.8
Wholesale, retail trade, and catering services	13.6	28.4	42.9	46.9	47.4	49.7
Banking and insurance	1.0	2.2	2.8	3.3	3.4	3.4
Real estate, social services, health, and education	18.5	26.3	27.0	30.7	31.5	31.8
Government, party agencies, and social organizations	5.3	10.8	10.4	11.0	11.0	10.8
Others	5.9	18.0	44.9	56.4	58.5	62.5
Residual[1]	1.1	81.2	58.3	92.8	101.4	102.1
Total	423.6	647.5	680.7	720.9	730.3	737.4
Primary	291.2	389.1	355.3	360.4	365.1	368.7
Nonagricultural	132.4	258.4	325.4	360.4	365.1	368.7
Secondary	77.1	138.6	156.6	162.2	162.8	157.8
Tertiary	55.3	119.8	168.8	198.2	202.3	210.9
	(In percent)					
Primary	68.7	60.1	52.2	50.0	50.0	50.0
Nonagricultural	31.3	39.9	47.8	50.0	50.0	50.0
Secondary	18.2	21.4	23.0	22.5	22.3	21.4
Tertiary	13.1	18.5	24.8	27.5	27.7	28.6

Sources: *China Statistical Yearbook*; and CEIC database.

[1]The residual is the difference between the aggregate employment figure from the household survey and the detail by industry from the establishment survey (which excludes much of the private sector).

River Delta (Guangdong) and Yangtze River Delta (Shanghai and Jiangsu) in particular, where job growth and incomes are relatively high (with GDP per capita 4 to 10 times that in poorer rural provinces such as Gansu and Guizhou). Estimates of the migrant population vary, ranging between 80 million and 150 million.[8]

The level of urban unemployment in China is similar to that of other countries in the region, but rural underemployment appears to be higher. Unemployment rates in most other Asian countries rose to about 3–6 percent following the 1997–98 financial crisis, similar to China's urban registered rate of 4 percent (excluding *xiagang*). In the rural sector, however, the low productivity of China's farmers compared with those in other Asian countries suggests a

higher level of underemployment than elsewhere in Asia (Table 8.4).

Labor Market Reforms

Progress on Reforms

The labor market has undergone significant changes since the opening up of the economy in the late 1970s. The prereform labor market was characterized by direct allocation of jobs and administrative control of wages. Employers had very little control over their workforce or the wage bill, and employees had little say in where they worked. China has gradually moved toward marketization of the labor market, particularly in the nonstate sector, including greater flexibility in hiring and firing of labor (Box 8.1).

Following the initiation of reforms in the early 1980s, a "dual-track transition" of the labor market took place with the development of the state sector. Employment in foreign-funded enterprises (FFEs) and collectives rose rapidly in the 1980s due to labor

---

[8]The National Bureau of Statistics estimates there were about 80 million permanent migrants (i.e., those living in urban areas for more than six months) between 1990 and 2000. No reliable data are available for the number of temporary migrants, with estimates in the range of 30–120 million.

Table 8.4. Selected Asian Economies: Labor Productivity, 2000[1]

	Agriculture/ Nonagriculture Productivity
China	0.19
Indonesia	0.25
Korea	0.40
Malaysia	0.42
Philippines	0.33
Taiwan Province of China	0.25

Sources: CEIC database; and author's estimates.
[1]Defined as value added divided by the number of employees.

market reforms and the opening of the economy to private and foreign investors. SOE employment also increased in the 1980s and early 1990s but at a more moderate pace.

As SOE reform gained pace in the late 1990s, about 24 million SOE and collective employees were laid off in 1998–2002 as part of a reemployment program (*xiagang*) that provided laid-off workers with a safety net. Such employees could enter reemployment centers (RECs) where they could stay until they found a job or for up to three years. As long as they stayed in the REC they remained officially employed by the SOE, but received a lower monthly benefit then their previous wage.[9] Although most of the *xiagang* are middle-aged workers with few skills and poor education, more than two-thirds were reported to have found jobs, while others have retired. The number of *xiagang* remaining in RECs has declined from a peak of about 9½ million at end-1999 to about 6.2 million by end-2002, as workers have found jobs, transferred to the registered unemployed, or dropped out of the workforce.

During the central planning period, control on population movement was achieved through a combination of household registration requirements (*hukou*), rural commune controls, and food rationing. The elimination of communes and the emergence of a free market for grain and essential food items in the 1980s reduced obstacles to rural-urban migration. *Hukou* reforms were initiated in the 1990s, but more significant steps were only taken in 2003 (Box 8.2). However, other barriers to internal migration still exist, such as fees and charges on rural migrants, a prohibi-

---

[9]In 2002, average payments to *xiagang* were around 35–40 percent of the average earnings for workers in the manufacturing sector.

Box 8.1. Steps Toward Labor Market Flexibility

In 1980, China's first national work conference on labor market issues adopted a strategy for fostering a more flexible labor market. Urban job seekers were allowed to find work in the state, collective, or newly recognized private sectors, and enterprises were granted more autonomy in hiring decisions. The authorities, however, continued to formulate a labor plan, but instead of unilaterally allocating workers to enterprises, labor bureaus began to match job seekers with work units that wanted additional labor.

Wage flexibility has been increased gradually. From 1978, firms were allowed to reinstitute bonuses (subject to ceilings) and piece wages. In 1994, the introduction of a new Labor Law also gave management more discretion over wage determination. As a result of these reforms, the share of bonuses in total wages for all enterprises rose from 2 percent of the wage bill at the start of the reforms in 1978 to about 16 percent in 1997.

A labor contracting system was introduced in the mid-1980s. This signaled a marked shift away from the system of lifetime tenures with its potentially distorted work incentives. The initial steps were modest and resulted in only moderate growth in the share of employees under contract, but further reforms in 1994 gave new impetus to labor contracting. As a result, the share of workers on contracts almost doubled between 1994 and 1997, to about one-third of urban workers. Restrictions on movements of workers across firms were also removed, in an attempt to reduce the scale of the mismatch of labor inherent in the pre-reform system.

SOEs gained the right to lay off permanent workers. Those employees without contracts had lifetime tenure with SOEs, but in the mid-1990s, this presumption of tenure was eroded. SOEs, however, were required to established so-called reemployment centers (RECs) for laid-off workers (*xiagang*), which provide retraining and job search assistance and pay unemployment benefits. If the laid-off worker remained unemployed for more than three years, the employer could sever the relationship. From 2002, newly laid-off workers receive only unemployment benefits, and the RECs will be phased out by 2004.

tion on rural migrants working in certain sectors, and uncertainties about the portability of pensions and health insurance across regions.

Remaining Challenges

Despite the considerable progress made on reforms in the past two decades, surplus labor

Box 8.2. *Hukou* Reform

The household registration (*hukou*) system was set up in the mid-1950s to control the movement of the population and effectively constrained the development of a national labor market. An urban *hukou* was needed to stay in cities and gain preferential access to city services such as education, health, and social security. Moreover, urban enterprises were restricted from recruiting labor from another province unless labor could not be found locally.

Since the mid-1990s, reforms to the *hukou* system have been initiated. In 1997, the authorities experimented with relaxation of household registration regulations in some small towns and cities, allowing migrants who had either a stable income (from a job or business) or owned a house to obtain an "urban *hukou*." These reforms, however, were not very far-reaching, and, by end-2000, only 540,000 people had applied for a *hukou* in small towns and cities.

The reform gained momentum in 2001. Since October 2001, a person with stable work and a residence should be able to obtain a *hukou* in more than 20,000 small towns and cities, while retaining land use rights in the countryside. In addition, the State Planning Commission stipulated that charges levied by localities on migrants, such as "temporary residence fees" and "birth control fees," must be removed by early 2002. These charges could amount to several hundred renminbi, a sizable portion of migrant earnings. Guangdong province led the way by abolishing the division between agricultural and nonagricultural categories of *hukou*. A further loosening of the *hukou* system was announced in August 2003 by the Ministry of Public Security to encourage the movement of labor to less-developed regions. Professionals who work in small towns or rural areas or who migrate to invest or work in undeveloped western regions may retain their original urban household registration.

While the new reforms are a significant step toward establishing a national labor market, a number of barriers remain. First, a *hukou* in small towns and cities is not as attractive to rural migrants as a *hukou* in large and medium-sized cities (that provide better services), where reforms have not been as far reaching. Second, the ownership of a residence is a demanding condition for most rural migrants to meet, given their relatively low income. Third, access to social services, such as education, welfare, and pensions, remains a problem for migrants as they are generally required to return to their place of permanent residence to receive these services, or face sizable fees for services in their adopted home city. Fourth, localities will likely resist removing fees applied to migrants, given the potential loss of revenue. Fifth, those who obtain an urban *hukou* can give birth to only one child, while in many rural areas, two children are permitted.

remains in SOEs and on farms. Labor productivity of SOEs still lags behind the nonstate sector, suggesting that, if SOE labor productivity could be raised to nonstate levels, about 10–11 million SOE workers could be considered redundant (Table 8.5).[10]

A large labor surplus also persists on the farms, despite the already sizable flow of migrants from the farms to the cities. The Organization for Economic Cooperation and Development (OECD, 2002b) estimates that, if the average GDP contribution per worker in nonagricultural jobs is used as a benchmark, rural hidden unemployment can be estimated to represent around 275 million (where hidden unemployment is defined as low-productive employment regardless of working time). If the benchmark is set more modestly at one-third of the productivity of nonagricultural workers (in line with other Asian countries), rural hidden unemployment would be around 150 million.

Labor market pressures are also coming from accession to WTO. Li and Zhai (1999) estimate that gross job losses as a result of WTO accession could amount to about 14½ million, comprising 13 million workers in rural areas and 1½ million in urban areas (mainly in the automobile and machinery industries). On the other hand, the textile and clothing industry, in particular, will get a boost from 2005 onward with the elimination of quotas, and its strong cost competitiveness may lead to a sizable increase in China's world market share (see Martin and others, 1999). Job growth, therefore, could be enhanced by facilitating a shift of resources from less competitive capital-intensive industries, such as transport and heavy machinery, toward more labor-intensive sectors, such as textiles and clothing, and services.[11]

---

[10]In 2001, labor productivity of SOEs in the industrial sector was only 71 percent of nonstate enterprises, suggesting that (from a partial equilibrium perspective), if SOE labor productivity matched that of non-SOEs, almost one-third of the 15½ million SOE workers in this sector could be redundant. Given that a further 22 million SOE workers are employed outside the industrial sector, this implies a total SOE labor surplus of about 10–11 million. Labor productivity in foreign-funded enterprises is almost twice that of SOEs, suggesting that, if this higher benchmark were used, almost half the SOE workers (or 18 million) could be considered redundant.

---

[11]For example, if output of the textile and clothing industry increased by 50 percent while automobile and ordinary machinery output fell by 50 percent, the net increase in jobs would be about 1 million due to the labor intensive nature of the textile and clothing industry (assuming no changes in labor productivity in either sector; both sectors had a similar level of output in 2000).

Table 8.5. Industrial Employment and Output

	1995	1997	1999	2000	2001
Industrial sector					
Value added (billions renminbi)	1,942.0	1,983.5	2,156.4	2,539.2	2,832.9
Employees (millions)	66.1	78.7	58.1	55.8	54.4
Output/employee (thousands of renminbi)	29.4	25.2	37.1	45.5	52.1
State-owned					
Value added	1,107.0	919.2	820.4	721.3	623.4
Employees	43.9	38.9	25.1	19.7	15.4
Output/employee	25.2	23.6	32.7	36.6	40.4
Non-state-owned					
Value added	835.0	1,064.3	1,336.0	1,817.9	2,209.5
Employees	22.2	39.8	33.0	36.1	39.0
Output/employee	37.6	26.7	40.5	50.4	56.7
Ratio, state to non-state-owned					
Value added	1.33	0.86	0.61	0.40	0.28
Employees	1.98	0.98	0.76	0.55	0.39
Output/employee	0.67	0.88	0.81	0.73	0.71
Selected categories					
Foreign funded (including Hong Kong SAR, Macao SAR, and Taiwan Province of China)					
Value added	228.1	354.0	485.0	609.0	712.8
Employees	4.8	7.1	7.9	8.5	9.4
Output/employee	47.5	49.9	61.4	71.6	75.8
Textiles, garments, leather, and furs					
Value added	144.6	187.1	190.5	218.9	246.7
Employees	9.5	11.1	8.2	8.1	8.4
Output/employee	15.3	16.9	23.2	26.9	29.4
Transportation equipment and ordinary machinery					
Value added	147.4	180.0	193.7	216.5	260.5
Employees	7.8	8.2	5.3	5.1	5.7
Output/employee	19.0	22.0	36.5	42.1	45.7

Sources: *China Industrial Statistical Yearbook*; and author's estimates.

The relatively low skill levels of rural labor and the urban unemployed make it more difficult for them to find quality jobs. Illiteracy rates are much higher among the rural population, with relatively few rural residents having completed secondary school or college.[12] Skill levels are also low in the northeastern provinces of Heilongjiang, Jilin, and Liaoning where there is a higher-than-average concentration of unemployed and *xiagang*. In these provinces, only about one in five people have education beyond junior-middle school.

The authorities are moving to improve training and education of the largely unskilled *xiagang* and migrants. The World Bank (2001) notes that a variety of government programs have increased the poor's access to education in the 1990s, including an effort to achieve nine-year universal basic education by 2010. However, funding is inadequate in many poorer regions.

Given the pressures on the labor market, the government has been strengthening the social safety net outside of RECs for urban workers. An unemployment insurance fund has been established, separate from the RECs, and now covers more than 100 million urban workers (about 40 percent of the urban workforce). It is a defined-benefit system funded by mandatory contributions from employers (2 percent of payroll) and employees (1 percent of salary), with

---

[12]Illiteracy exceeded 15 percent of the population (aged 15 and above) in six predominantly rural western provinces (Guizhou, Gansu, Ningxia, Qinghai, Tibet, and Yunan) in 2000 but was less than 5 percent in many of the more urbanized eastern provinces. In the same western provinces, the proportion of the population (aged 6 and above) with education beyond junior-middle school was less than 15 percent, while in the eastern provinces of Beijing, Tianjing, and Shanghai it was much higher, in the range of 30–40 percent.

Table 8.6. Estimates of Elasticity of Nonagricultural Employment Growth to Output Growth[1]

(Dependent variable: Δ log (provincial employment))

Variable	National	Eastern Provinces	Mid and Western Provinces	1978–93	1993–2000
Δ log (provincial GDP)	0.38	0.43	0.35	0.47	0.30
	(17.90)	(12.70)	(5.35)	(21.10)	(5.75)
Δ log (provincial wages)	−0.01	−0.06	0.00	0.01	−0.22
	(0.51)	(0.54)	(0.03)	(1.21)	(4.2)
No. of observations	636	257	379	426	210
Adjusted R-squared	0.07	0.10	0.09	0.09	0.10

Sources: Author's estimates.

[1]A panel regression was undertaken, including provincial dummies and time dummies to control for unobservable effects, using the following specification (with absolute t-statistics in parentheses):

$\Delta \log (Employment_{it}) = \alpha \, \Delta \log (GDP_{it}) + \beta \, \Delta \log (wages_{it})$ + province dummies + time dummies + ϵ_{it}, where $Employment_{it}$ is total employment in nonagricultural sectors of the province i in year t; GDP is nonagricultural GDP (deflated by the GDP deflator) of province i in year t; wages is the nominal wage index deflated by the CPI of the province in year t, and Δ is the first difference operator.

benefits lasting 12–24 months.[13] However, actual contribution rates vary depending on the local unemployment situation, which has amplified regional disparities as firms and workers in areas with weaker economic growth have to contribute more. National pooling of the unemployment fund would help reduce such disparities. Minimum wage legislation was also introduced with the new Labor Law in 1993. Minimum wage standards have been established in all provinces, but the government has faced difficulties in enforcing compliance, especially for migrant workers.

Some Illustrative Projections

Looking ahead, the capacity of the labor market to absorb the 160 million or so surplus workers in the rural and SOE sectors can be assessed by analyzing a range of projections for labor supply and demand. Econometric estimates based on provincial level data suggest that a 1 percent increase in GDP is correlated with a 0.4 percent increase in nonagricultural employment in the past two decades (Table 8.6).[14]

[13]Twelve months for those who contributed 1–5 years, 18 months for those who contributed 5–10 years, and 24 months for those who contributed more than 10 years.

[14]Panel regressions were estimated for nonagricultural employment growth data by province over the period 1978–2000. The equations (estimated in double-log form) specify provincial nonagricultural employment as a function of output growth, real wage growth, and provincial and time dummies. The provincial data are subject to large measurement errors owing to statistical weaknesses in the provincial GDP and employment data. See Brooks and Ran (2003) for more details on the data and estimation.

The elasticity appears to be somewhat higher in the eastern provinces (about 0.43), where there is a greater concentration of private sector firms. The elasticity was lower in the late 1990s (about 0.3), as SOEs moved to cut labor and lift productivity.

Specifically, a central scenario assumes the following:

(1) The working age population grows by 11–12 million annually through 2006, before slowing thereafter, based on projections by Wang (2001).

(2) The labor force participation rate stays at the 2002 level of 83 percent.

(3) All new entrants to the labor force seek jobs in the nonagricultural sector.

(4) Nonagricultural GDP grows by 7½ percent annually through 2010 (implying overall GDP growth of about 7 percent).

(5) The elasticity of employment growth to output growth is 0.45 percent.

(6) The impact of wage growth on employment is relatively minor.

Projections for the central scenario of nonagricultural growth of 7½ percent suggest that unemployment could rise in the coming years (Table 8.7). New job growth is projected at about 12–13 million annually in 2004–2006, before taking account of future SOE downsizing. This is somewhat higher than the 8 million average annual increase in 1995–2002, which was held down by SOE job losses. Most of the new jobs are assumed to be taken by new entrants to the labor force (9–10 million annually). This implies that the labor market can absorb about 3–4 million surplus rural and SOE workers annually in 2004–

Table 8.7. Labor Force and Employment Projections[1]

(In millions)

	2002	2003 (est.)	2004	2005	2006	2010	Sum for 2004–06	Sum for 2004–10
Nonagricultural employment	357[2]	366	378	391	404	461	...	...
New jobs (annual increase)	...	9	12	13	13	15	38	96
Total population	1,285	1,292	1,300	1,308	1,315	1,342	...	...
Working age population (15–64)	903	916	927	939	951	988	...	...
Increase of working age population (annual change)	9	13	11	12	11	8	34	72
Increase of labor force (annual change)	9	11	9	10	9	7	29	60
New jobs less increase in labor force	...	−2	3	3	4	8	10	36
Surplus labor seeking jobs	...	2	9	9	7	5	25	50
SOE reemployment	...	1	3	3	2	0	8	10
Rural migrants	...	1	6	6	5	5	17	40
Change in urban unemployment (survey based)[3]	...	4	6	6	3	−3	15	14
Urban unemployment rate (in percent)[4]	4.5	5.8	7.7	9.7	10.4	9.0		

Sources: Author's estimates.

[1] Assuming 7 percent GDP growth, 7½ percent nonagricultural GDP growth, and 0.45 employment elasticity.

[2] End-2002 employment is reduced by 11 million to take account of remaining redundant SOE workers.

[3] Defined as surplus labor seeking jobs less new jobs less increase in labor force.

[4] The urban unemployment rate for 2002 is based on the survey data referred to by the NBS Commissioner in October 2002.

2006, without increasing the explicit urban unemployment rate. However, if most of the SOE downsizing takes place in the next three years, and about 6 million rural migrants[15] move to urban areas annually, the unemployment rate (survey based) could more than double to a peak of over 10 percent by 2005. The unemployment rate would then decline to below 10 percent by 2010, as the natural increase in the labor force slows and SOE downsizing is completed.

Using more optimistic assumptions of 8½ percent nonagricultural growth and an employment elasticity of 0.6 (assuming growth is led by the labor-intensive service sector) implies that the nonagricultural economy could absorb over 90 million surplus workers in 2004–10, more than half of the rural and SOE labor surplus (Table 8.8). A more pessimistic scenario of 6½ percent nonagricultural growth and an employment elasticity of 0.30 (assuming that growth is led by capital-intensive sectors) suggests that labor force growth would outstrip job growth in 2004–10 by 7 million, putting considerable upward pressure on unemployment. The unemployment projection also depends crucially on the assumption about migra-

tion, with rural migrants unlikely to come to urban areas unless jobs are available. Therefore, the urban unemployment rate may not rise significantly if

Table 8.8. Projections of Jobs for Migrants and Laid-Off Workers from SOEs[1]

A. 2004–06 job increase, in millions

Assumptions:		Growth rate (in percent)[2]		
		6.5	7.5	8.5
Employment growth	0.30	−7	−3	0
Elasticity	0.45	5	10	15
	0.60	16	23	30

B. 2004–10 job increase, in millions

Assumptions:		Growth rate (in percent)[2]		
		6.5	7.5	8.5
Employment growth	0.30	−7	2	11
Elasticity	0.45	22	36	50
	0.60	53	72	93

Source: Author's estimates.

[1] Defined as new jobs less the increase in the labor force due to growth in the working age population.

[2] For the nonagricultural sector. Roughly equivalent to 6, 7, and 8 percent, respectively, for overall GDP growth.

---

[15] About three-quarters of the annual rate indicated in the Tenth Five-Year plan, which targeted the transfer of 40 million rural labor force into urban areas over the period 2001–2005.

migrants remain on the farms as part of the surplus rural labor.

These projections are of course only illustrative and are subject to a wide range of uncertainty. Nevertheless, they indicate the magnitude of the challenges that lie ahead in absorbing unemployed and underemployed persons into the workforce.

The Road Ahead

The labor market has become more market oriented over the past twenty years, and the main challenge now is to create quality jobs for the new entrants to the labor force as well as absorb the sizable labor surplus in the SOE and rural sectors. To address the labor market pressures, government policies have begun to focus on encouraging job growth in the private sector (especially in the service sector), which has been the main source of job growth in recent years. Indeed, the third plenum of the Six-teenth Congress of the Communist Party in late 2003 stressed the need to support private sector development to create employment. Removing the numerous hurdles to growth that are still faced by private firms is therefore a crucial priority for fostering job creation.

The government is also considering a further liberalization of the *hukou* system of residency permits, which would be needed to allow surplus rural workers to move to the cities and allow unemployed and *xiagang* in low-job-growth regions to relocate to higher-growth regions. This reform would also help to address the widening gap between urban and rural incomes. Other challenges that remain to improve the functioning of the labor market include enhancing worker skills, providing easier access to information on job opportunities and fostering the establishment of private employment agencies, and strengthening the unemployment insurance scheme and other social safety nets to help protect vulnerable groups.

References

Adhikari, Ramesh, and Yongzheng Yang, 2002, "What Will WTO Membership Mean for China and Its Trading Partners?" *Finance and Development,* Vol. 39, No. 3, September, pp. 22–25.

Ahmad, Ehtisham, 1997, "China," in *Fiscal Federalism in Theory and Practice,* ed. by Teresa Ter-Minassian (Washington: International Monetary Fund).

———, Li Keping, Thomas Richardson, and Raju Singh, 2002, "Recentralization in China?" IMF Working Paper No. 02/168 (Washington: International Monetary Fund).

Ahmad, Ehtisham, Mario Fortuna, and Raju Singh, 2004, "Towards More Effective Redistribution: Reform Options for Intergovernmental Transfers in China" IMF Working Paper, forthcoming (Washington: International Monetary Fund).

Ahmed, Shaghil, 2003, "Sources of Economic Fluctuations in Latin America and Implications for Choice of Exchange Rate Regimes," *Journal of Development Economics,* Vol. 72, No.1 (October), pp. 181–202.

Alberola, Enrique, Susana G. Cervero, J. Humberto Lopez, and Angel Ubide, 1999, "Global Equilibrium Exchange Rates—Euro, Dollar, 'Ins,' 'Outs,' and Other Major Currencies in a Panel Cointegration Framework," IMF Working Paper No. 99/175 (Washington: International Monetary Fund).

Balassa, Bela, 1964, "The Purchasing Power Parity Doctrine: A Reappraisal," *Journal of Political Economy,* Vol. 72 (December), pp. 584–96.

Banker, 2003, "Top 1000 World Banks," Vol. 153, Issue 929 (July), p. 143.

Bayoumi, Tamim, Hamid Faruqee, and Jaewoo Lee, 2003, "A Fair Exchange? Theory and Practice of Calculating Underlying Exchange Rate Trends" (unpublished; Washington: International Monetary Fund).

Bell, Michael W., Hoe Ee Khor, and Kalpana Kochhar, 1993, *China at the Threshold of a Market Economy,* IMF Occasional Paper No. 107 (Washington: International Monetary Fund).

Blanchard, Olivier, and Danny Quah, 1989, "The Dynamic Effects of Aggregate Demand and Supply Disturbances," *American Economic Review,* Vol. 79 (September), pp. 655–73.

Blanchard, Olivier, and Andrei Shleifer, 2001, "Federalism With and Without Political Centralization: China Versus Russia," *IMF Staff Papers,* Vol. 48 (Special Issue), pp. 171–79.

Borda, Patrice, Olivier Manioc, and Jean Gabriel Montauban, 2000, "The Contribution of U.S. Monetary Policy to Caribbean Business Cycles," *Social and Economic Studies,* Vol. 49 (Special Issue), June/September, pp. 225–50.

Bottelier, Pieter, 2002, "Implications of WTO Membership for China's State-Owned Banks and the Management of Public Finances: Issues and Strategies," paper presented at the Annual Meetings of the Asian Development Bank, Shanghai.

Brooks, Ray, and Ran Tao, 2003, "China's Labor Market Performance and Challenges," IMF Working Paper No. 03/210 (Washington: International Monetary Fund).

Cai, F., W. Dewen, and D. Yang, 2001 "Labor Market Distortions and Economic Growth: Examining Institutional Components of Regional Disparity in China," Working Paper No. 10 (Beijing: Center for Human Resource Studies, Chinese Academy of Social Sciences).

Chadha, Bankim, and Eswar Prasad, 1997, "Real Exchange Rate Fluctuations and the Business Cycle: Evidence from Japan," *IMF Staff Papers,* Vol. 44, No. 3 (September), pp. 328–55.

Chen, Show-Lin, and Jyh-Lin Wu, 1997, "Sources of Real Exchange Rate Fluctuations: Empirical Evidence from Four Pacific Basin Countries," *Southern Economic Journal,* Vol. 63 (January), pp. 776–87.

China Finance Yearbook, various issues.

China Industrial Statistical Year Book, various years.

China Statistical Year Book, various years.

Chinn, Menzie, and Eswar S. Prasad, 2003, "Medium-Term Determinants of Current Accounts in Industrial and Developing Countries: An Empirical Exploration," *Journal of International Economics,* Vol. 59, No. 1 (January), pp. 47–76.

Chou, W.L, and Y.C. Shih, 1998, "The Equilibrium Exchange Rate of the Chinese Renminbi," *Journal of Comparative Economics,* Vol. 26 (March), pp. 165–74.

Clarida, Richard, and Jordi Gali, 1994, "Sources of Real Exchange Rate Fluctuations: How Important Are Nominal Shocks?" NBER Working Paper No. 4658 (Cambridge, Massachusetts: National Bureau of Economic Research).

Daniel, James, Tom Richardson, Raju Jan Singh, and George Tsibouris, 2003, "Medium-Term Fiscal Issues," in *China: Competing in the Global Economy— Policies for Sustained Growth and Financial Stability,* ed. by Wanda Tseng and Markus Rodlauer (Washington: International Monetary Fund).

Dibooglu, Selahattin, and Ali M. Kutan, 2001, "Sources of Real Exchange Rate Fluctuations in Transition

Economies: The Case of Poland and Hungary," *Journal of Comparative Economics,* Vol. 29, No. 2 (June), pp. 257–75.

Dorfman, Mark, and Yee Mun Sin, 2001, "China: Social Security Reform—Strategic Options" (unpublished; Washington: World Bank).

Findlay, Christopher, Harry X. Wu, and Andrew Watson, 1995, "Fiscal Decentralisation, Regionalism and Uneven Development in China," Chinese Economy Research Unit Working Paper No. 95/5 (Adelaide, Australia: University of Adelaide).

Funke, Michael, and Jörg Rahn, 2004, "By How Much Is the Chinese Renminbi Undervalued?" (unpublished; Hamburg: Hamburg University).

Hertel, Thomas, and Terrie Walmsley, 2000, "China's Accession to the WTO: Timing Is Everything" (West Lafayette, Indiana: Center for Global Trade Analysis, Purdue University).

Hoffmaister, Alexander W., and Jorge E. Roldós, 2001, "The Sources of Macroeconomic Fluctuations in Developing Countries: Brazil and Korea," *Journal of Macroeconomics,* Vol. 23, No. 2 (Spring), pp. 213–39.

Ianchovichina, Elena, and Will Martin, 2003, "Economic Impacts of China's Accession to the World Trade Organization," Policy Research Working Paper No. 3053 (Washington: World Bank).

Isard, Peter, and Hamid Faruqee, eds., 1998, *Exchange Rate Assessment: Extensions of the Macroeconomic Balance Approach,* IMF Occasional Paper No. 167 (Washington: International Monetary Fund).

———, G. Russell Kincaid, and Martin Fetherston, 2001, *Methodology for Current Account and Exchange Rate Assessments,* IMF Occasional Paper No. 209 (Washington: International Monetary Fund).

Jin, Hehui, Yingyi Qian, and Barry Weingast, 2003a, "Federalism, Chinese Style I: Fiscal Incentives and Regional Development" (unpublished; Oakland, California: University of California, Berkeley).

———, 2003b, "Federalism, Chinese Style II: Economic Decentralization and Political Decentralization" (unpublished; Oakland, California: University of California, Berkeley).

Karacadag, Cem, 2003, "Financial System Soundness and Reform," in *China: Competing in the Global Economy,* ed. by Wanda Tseng and Markus Rodlauer (Washington: International Monetary Fund).

Lane, Philip R., and Gian Maria Milesi-Ferretti, 2000, "The Transfer Problem Revisited: Net Foreign Assets and Real Exchange Rates," IMF Working Paper No. 00/123 (Washington: International Monetary Fund).

Lardy, Nicolas R., 1998, *China's Unfinished Economic Revolution* (Washington: Brookings Institution).

———, 2000, "Fiscal Sustainability: Between a Rock and a Hard Place," *China Economic Quarterly,* pp. 36–41.

———, 2002, *Integrating China into the Global Economy* (Washington: Brookings Institution).

Li, S., and F. Zhai, 1999, "China's WTO Accession and Implications for National and Provincial Economies" (unpublished).

Martin, W., B. Dimaranan, and T. Hertel, 1999, "Trade Policies, Structural Changes and China's Trade Growth" (unpublished).

Mattoo, Aaditya, 2002, "China's Accession to the WTO: The Services Dimension," World Bank Policy Research Working Paper No. 2932 (Washington: World Bank).

Ministry of Finance, 2002, "Accounting Information Quality Assessment Report," People's Republic of China.

National Audit Office of the People's Republic of China, 2002, *Audit Report.*

Nehru, Vikram, and others, 1997, *China 2020—Development Challenges in the New Century* (Washington: World Bank).

Organization for Economic Cooperation and Development (OECD), 2002a, *Realizing the Benefits of China's Trade and Investment Liberalization: The Domestic Economic Policy Challenges* (Paris).

———, 2002b, *China in the World Economy: the Domestic Policy Challenges* (Paris).

Panitchpakdi, Supachai, and Mark L. Clifford, 2002, "China and the WTO: Changing China, Changing World Trade" (Singapore: John Wiley & Sons (Asia)).

Prasad, Eswar, and Thomas Rumbaugh, 2003, "Beyond the Great Wall," *Finance and Development,* Vol. 40, No. 4 (December), pp. 46–49.

Qiang, Gao, and Barry Weingast, 1997, "Federalism as a Commitment to Preserving Market Incentives," *Journal of Economic Perspectives,* Vol. 11 (Fall), pp. 83–92.

Rumbaugh, Thomas, and Nicolas Blancher, 2004, "China: International Trade and WTO Accession," IMF Working Paper No. 04/36 (Washington: International Monetary Fund).

Solinger, Dorothy J., 2002, "Special Report: China's Employment Mess," *China Economic Quarterly,* No. 4.

Steinfeld, Edward S., 2000, *Forging Reform in China* (New York: Cambridge University Press).

Studwell, Joe, 2000, "On the Block: What Is the Family Silver Worth?" *China Economic Quarterly,* No. 2.

Tenev, Stoyan, Chunlin Zhang, and Loup Brefort, 2002, *Corporate Governance and Enterprise Reform in China: Building the Institutions of Modern Markets* (Washington: World Bank and International Finance Corporation).

Tseng, Wanda, Hoe Ee Khor, Kalpana Kochhar, Dubravko Mihaljek, and David Burton, 1994, *Economic Reform in China: A New Phase,* IMF Occasional Paper No. 114 (Washington: International Monetary Fund).

Tseng, Wanda, and Markus Rodlauer, eds., 2003, *China: Competing in the Global Economy—Policies for Sustained Growth and Financial Stability* (Washington: International Monetary Fund).

United States Trade Representative, 2002, *Report to Congress on China's WTO Compliance,* December.

Wang, G., 2001, "Projections of China's Population from 2001–10," working paper presented at a conference on "China Labor Markets in Transition," December.

Wang, Tao, 2004, "China: Sources of Real Exchange Rate Fluctuations," IMF Working Paper

No. 04/18 (Washington: International Monetary Fund).

Wong, Christine P., ed., 1997, *Financing Local Government in the People's Republic of China* (Hong Kong SAR; New York: Oxford University Press).

World Bank, 2001, *China: Overcoming Rural Poverty* (Washington: World Bank).

———, 2002, *China—Provincial Expenditure Review,* January (Washington: World Bank).

———, 2003, *China—Promoting Growth with Equity*, Country Economic Memorandum, September (Washington: World Bank).

Yang, Yongzheng, 2003, "China's Integration into the World Economy: Implications for Developing Countries," IMF Working Paper No. 03/245 (Washington: International Monetary Fund).

Young, Alwyn, 2000a, "The Razor's Edge: Distortions and Incremental Reform in the People's Republic of China," *Quarterly Journal of Economics,* Vol. 105, No. 4 (November), pp. 1091–1135.

———, 2000b, "Gold into Base Metals: Productivity Growth in the People's Republic of China During the Reform Period," NBER Working Paper No. 7856 (Cambridge, Massachusetts: National Bureau of Economic Research).

Zhang, Zhichao, 2001, "Real Exchange Rate Misalignment in China: An Empirical Investigation," *Journal of Comparative Economics,* Vol. 29, No. 1 (March), pp. 80–94.

Zhao, Yaohui, 2001, paper presented at a seminar on "Economic Reform and the Labor Market in China," December.

Recent Occasional Papers of the International Monetary Fund

232. China's Growth and Integration into the World Economy: Prospects and Challenges, edited by Eswar Prasad, 2004.

231. Chile: Institutions and Policies Underpinning Stability and Growth, by Eliot Kalter, Steven Phillips, Marco A. Espinosa-Vega, Rodolfo Luzio, Mauricio Villafuerte, and Manmohan Singh. 2004.

230. Financial Stability in Dollarized Countries, by Anne-Marie Gulde, David Hoelscher, Alain Ize, David Marston, and Gianni De Nicoló. 2004.

229. Evolution and Performance of Exchange Rate Regimes, by Kenneth S. Rogoff, Aasim M. Husain, Ashoka Mody, Robin Brooks, and Nienke Oomes. 2004.

228. Capital Markets and Financial Intermediation in The Baltics, by Alfred Schipke, Christian Beddies, Susan M. George, and Niamh Sheridan. 2004.

227. U.S. Fiscal Policies and Priorities for Long-Run Sustainability, Martin Mühleisen and Christopher Towe, editors. 2004.

226. Hong Kong SAR: Meeting the Challenges of Integration with the Mainland, edited by Eswar Prasad, with contributions from Jorge Chan-Lau, Dora Iakova, William Lee, Hong Liang, Ida Liu, Papa N'Diaye, and Tao Wang. 2004.

225. Rules-Based Fiscal Policy in France, Germany, Italy, and Spain, by Teresa Dában, Enrica Detragiache, Gabriel di Bella, Gian Maria Milesi-Ferretti, and Steven Symansky. 2003.

224. Managing Systemic Banking Crises, by a staff team led by David S. Hoelscher and Marc Quintyn. 2003.

223. Monetary Union Among Member Countries of the Gulf Cooperation Council, by a staff team led by Ugo Fasano. 2003.

222. Informal Funds Transfer Systems: An Analysis of the Informal Hawala System, by Mohammed El Qorchi, Samuel Munzele Maimbo, and John F. Wilson. 2003.

221. Deflation: Determinants, Risks, and Policy Options, by Manmohan S. Kumar. 2003.

220. Effects of Financial Globalization on Developing Countries: Some Empirical Evidence, by Eswar S. Prasad, Kenneth Rogoff, Shang-Jin Wei, and Ayhan Kose. 2003.

219. Economic Policy in a Highly Dollarized Economy: The Case of Cambodia, by Mario de Zamaroczy and Sopanha Sa. 2003.

218. Fiscal Vulnerability and Financial Crises in Emerging Market Economies, by Richard Hemming, Michael Kell, and Axel Schimmelpfennig. 2003.

217. Managing Financial Crises: Recent Experience and Lessons for Latin America, edited by Charles Collyns and G. Russell Kincaid. 2003.

216. Is the PRGF Living Up to Expectations?—An Assessment of Program Design, by Sanjeev Gupta, Mark Plant, Benedict Clements, Thomas Dorsey, Emanuele Baldacci, Gabriela Inchauste, Shamsuddin Tareq, and Nita Thacker. 2002.

215. Improving Large Taxpayers' Compliance: A Review of Country Experience, by Katherine Baer. 2002.

214. Advanced Country Experiences with Capital Account Liberalization, by Age Bakker and Bryan Chapple. 2002.

213. The Baltic Countries: Medium-Term Fiscal Issues Related to EU and NATO Accession, by Johannes Mueller, Christian Beddies, Robert Burgess, Vitali Kramarenko, and Joannes Mongardini. 2002.

212. Financial Soundness Indicators: Analytical Aspects and Country Practices, by V. Sundararajan, Charles Enoch, Armida San José, Paul Hilbers, Russell Krueger, Marina Moretti, and Graham Slack. 2002.

211. Capital Account Liberalization and Financial Sector Stability, by a staff team led by Shogo Ishii and Karl Habermeier. 2002.

210. IMF-Supported Programs in Capital Account Crises, by Atish Ghosh, Timothy Lane, Marianne Schulze-Ghattas, Aleš Bulíř, Javier Hamann, and Alex Mourmouras. 2002.

209. Methodology for Current Account and Exchange Rate Assessments, by Peter Isard, Hamid Faruqee, G. Russell Kincaid, and Martin Fetherston. 2001.

208. Yemen in the 1990s: From Unification to Economic Reform, by Klaus Enders, Sherwyn Williams, Nada Choueiri, Yuri Sobolev, and Jan Walliser. 2001.

207. Malaysia: From Crisis to Recovery, by Kanitta Meesook, Il Houng Lee, Olin Liu, Yougesh Khatri, Natalia Tamirisa, Michael Moore, and Mark H. Krysl. 2001.

206. The Dominican Republic: Stabilization, Structural Reform, and Economic Growth, by a staff team led by PhilipYoung comprising Alessandro Giustiniani, Werner C. Keller, and Randa E. Sab and others. 2001.

205. Stabilization and Savings Funds for Nonrenewable Resources, by Jeffrey Davis, Rolando Ossowski, James Daniel, and Steven Barnett. 2001.

204. Monetary Union in West Africa (ECOWAS): Is It Desirable and How Could It Be Achieved? by Paul Masson and Catherine Pattillo. 2001.

203. Modern Banking and OTC Derivatives Markets: The Transformation of Global Finance and Its Implications for Systemic Risk, by Garry J. Schinasi, R. Sean Craig, Burkhard Drees, and Charles Kramer. 2000.

202. Adopting Inflation Targeting: Practical Issues for Emerging Market Countries, by Andrea Schaechter, Mark R. Stone, and Mark Zelmer. 2000.

201. Developments and Challenges in the Caribbean Region, by Samuel Itam, Simon Cueva, Erik Lundback, Janet Stotsky, and Stephen Tokarick. 2000.

200. Pension Reform in the Baltics: Issues and Prospects, by Jerald Schiff, Niko Hobdari, Axel Schimmelpfennig, and Roman Zytek. 2000.

199. Ghana: Economic Development in a Democratic Environment, by Sérgio Pereira Leite, Anthony Pellechio, Luisa Zanforlin, Girma Begashaw, Stefania Fabrizio, and Joachim Harnack. 2000.

198. Setting Up Treasuries in the Baltics, Russia, and Other Countries of the Former Soviet Union: An Assessment of IMF Technical Assistance, by Barry H. Potter and Jack Diamond. 2000.

197. Deposit Insurance: Actual and Good Practices, by Gillian G.H. Garcia. 2000.

196. Trade and Trade Policies in Eastern and Southern Africa, by a staff team led by Arvind Subramanian, with Enrique Gelbard, Richard Harmsen, Katrin Elborgh-Woytek, and Piroska Nagy. 2000.

195. The Eastern Caribbean Currency Union—Institutions, Performance, and Policy Issues, by Frits van Beek, José Roberto Rosales, Mayra Zermeño, Ruby Randall, and Jorge Shepherd. 2000.

194. Fiscal and Macroeconomic Impact of Privatization, by Jeffrey Davis, Rolando Ossowski, Thomas Richardson, and Steven Barnett. 2000.

193. Exchange Rate Regimes in an Increasingly Integrated World Economy, by Michael Mussa, Paul Masson, Alexander Swoboda, Esteban Jadresic, Paolo Mauro, and Andy Berg. 2000.

192. Macroprudential Indicators of Financial System Soundness, by a staff team led by Owen Evans, Alfredo M. Leone, Mahinder Gill, and Paul Hilbers. 2000.

191. Social Issues in IMF-Supported Programs, by Sanjeev Gupta, Louis Dicks-Mireaux, Ritha Khemani, Calvin McDonald, and Marijn Verhoeven. 2000.

190. Capital Controls: Country Experiences with Their Use and Liberalization, by Akira Ariyoshi, Karl Habermeier, Bernard Laurens, İnci Ötker-Robe, Jorge Iván Canales Kriljenko, and Andrei Kirilenko. 2000.

189. Current Account and External Sustainability in the Baltics, Russia, and Other Countries of the Former Soviet Union, by Donal McGettigan. 2000.

188. Financial Sector Crisis and Restructuring: Lessons from Asia, by Carl-Johan Lindgren, Tomás J.T. Baliño, Charles Enoch, Anne-Marie Gulde, Marc Quintyn, and Leslie Teo. 1999.

187. Philippines: Toward Sustainable and Rapid Growth, Recent Developments and the Agenda Ahead, by Markus Rodlauer, Prakash Loungani, Vivek Arora, Charalambos Christofides, Enrique G. De la Piedra, Piyabha Kongsamut, Kristina Kostial, Victoria Summers, and Athanasios Vamvakidis. 2000.

186. Anticipating Balance of Payments Crises: The Role of Early Warning Systems, by Andrew Berg, Eduardo Borensztein, Gian Maria Milesi-Ferretti, and Catherine Pattillo. 1999.

Note: For information on the titles and availability of Occasional Papers not listed, please consult the IMF's *Publications Catalog* or contact IMF Publication Services.